THE GATHERING STORM

4-1

The Gathering Storm

HAROLD LINDSELL

Tyndale House
Publishers, Inc.
Wheaton, Illinois

Scripture references, unless otherwise noted, are from the King James
Version of the Bible. Other Scriptures cited are from the *New International
Version* (NIV) Copyright © 1978 by the New York International Bible
Society; the *Revised Standard Version* (RSV) Copyright © 1952 by
the Division of Christian Education of the National Council of the Churches
of Christ in the United States of America; and *The Living Bible* (TLB)
Copyright © 1971 by Tyndale House Publishers.

CONTENTS

PREFACE

This book had its origins in a sermon I preached at the Park Street Church in Boston, Massachusetts, on Labor Day Sunday of 1979. When I finished preaching the sermon, I came to the conclusion that the subject itself was worth expanding into a book for several reasons. One was the indisputable fact that the signs of the times in this generation are markedly different from those which have prevailed throughout the history of the Christian Church. They appear to me to be signs which the Bible prophesies will characterize the last days.

The interest of the people who listened to the sermon and the questions which arose afterward led me to conclude that there is uncertainty and marked differences of opinion which need to be surfaced and talked about. Again and again the time of the rapture of the Church came to the fore, and I discovered that some of those who almost militantly favored the view that the Church will not go through the tribulation period did so because they did not wish to encounter the trials they would have to face. Their adherence to a pretribulation rapture viewpoint was based less on any rational defense of it from Scripture than on their personal wishes. I thought that the reasons why this is so and what the Scripture has to say should be studied more rigorously.

I have had wide contacts with people in the dispensational camp as well as wide contacts with people of the Reformed tradition. The former regard Israel and the Church as two separate and distinct entities with two different destinies. The latter hold that the Church is the New Israel and that the New Israel inherits what belonged to the old Israel. They do not distinguish Israel and the Church as distinct and separate entities. This needed to be looked into also.

The thorny question about a secret, any-moment rapture, by which there existed the possibility that Jesus could have returned for the Church at any time subsequent to Pentecost troubled me. I had difficulty aligning this with prophecies which seem to have been fulfilled recently and without which fulfillment the coming of the Lord could not occur. I found the writings of some of the leading dispensational brethren to be logically inconsistent. They claimed to believe that Jesus could rapture the Church at any moment. This provides no problem unless there are known predicted events which must take place *before* the Church is raptured. One of these predictions was the fall of Jerusalem which took place in A.D. 70. Thus, the Church could not have been raptured *before* that date, as we shall see later. Moreover, these same brethren wrote that the signs of the times showed that the rapture was close at hand. But if the rapture was imminent and any moment, then no signs would be important, nor could we talk about any signs in this generation.

I had recently completed a manuscript for a study edition of *The Living Bible* which is intended for release in November 1980. My studies forced me to spend time looking into the area of eschatology in order to write footnotes which would be helpful to all readers and which would offer the options available without dogmatically claiming to hold one or the other of alternate views which different Christians entertain. This examination of options had nothing to do with basic Christian truths which are not arguable, but with matters about which evangelical Christians have seen and still do see differently. I am a premillennialist and hold strongly to the fact that Scripture does teach there will be the rapture of the Church. I do not see how anyone can make a case against the rapture. I do see how people can be amillennialists or postmillennialists, although I think both of these options are untenable.

As I studied the subject of the second advent, I concluded that I did not wish to write a book which would detail the events connected with the end of the age. Many of these have already been written. The major topic under discussion for me was the rapidly multiplying evidences that we are entering into the closing days of this age and that the second advent of Jesus draws near. There is a risk in making a statement like that, for many people before my day have said the same thing and Jesus did not come. I may be wrong in my conclusion, and his coming may be delayed for another thousand years. But at least I wished to draw to the attention of evangelical Bible students who look for his coming the reasons why I think the last days are upon us.

Moreover, I have taken a hard look at the implications of the differing views about the time of the rapture and have come to see that one view has in it elements of which there should be a special awareness on the part of those who hold the view. They will be elaborated in the book.

Lastly, I have learned that, even though many hold a viewpoint in common, there are substantial differences among those who hold the same general position—differences which suggest that we need to be careful not to press our convictions too hard or too far for one particular position on the timing of the rapture.

I am convinced that Christ's victory over Satan must be consummated on earth even as sin was brought into human history on this planet. If there was a first Eden which was destroyed and paradise was lost, there must be a time when paradise will be regained and the Eden we lost will be seen here on earth, when the lion will lie down with the lamb, and when the swords of men will be beaten into plowshares and their spears into pruning hooks. This idyllic moment will not be brought to pass by wicked men who seem to grow worse rather than better. It will be brought to pass by the return of Jesus Christ who will establish his kingdom, sit on his throne, and rule over the nations of the world in peace and safety for all. If I die before that day dawns, I will be resurrected to see it with my own eyes. If it comes while I am still alive, I will be changed into his likeness and become what I would like to be but which I have not yet become.

Let us never forget that we see through the glass darkly, but the day is coming when we shall see things clearly and rightly.

Harold Lindsell
Wheaton, Illinois
February 1980

1
GOD AT WORK IN HISTORY

JESUS CHRIST HAS NOT COME AGAIN! ALMOST TWO thousand years have passed since he first uttered the words, "I will come again" (John 14:3). Generation after generation has lived and died and he has not come. During this period, enthusiasts have set specific times for his second advent and without exception all of them have been wrong.

He who said "of that day and hour knoweth no man" has confounded the would-be prophets again and again. Some of these so-called prophets, when proved to be in error, have introduced fanciful explanations to account for their disappointments. One thing stands out quite clearly in every instance when the time of his coming was forecast. He has not yet come, and history has not yet ended. Thus, those who were crestfallen when Jesus did not appear are still looking for the coming of the Lord in the same body with which he ascended into heaven forty days after his bodily resurrection from the dead.

One of the interesting and most widely held views among evangelicals has to do with a subsidiary question which is nonetheless dynamically related to the second advent. I refer to the rapture of the Church. Since the days of Darby, a Plymouth Brethren, the statement of the Apostle Paul in Titus "looking for that blessed hope, and the glorious appearing of the great God and our Saviour Jesus Christ" (2:13) has been understood to refer to the Church. In this view, the Church will be caught up or removed from the earth seven years (or more) prior to the second coming of Jesus Christ to earth. These seven years just prior to the coming of Jesus Christ will comprise the period known as the tribulation of which the last three and a half years is known as the great tribulation. The name applied to this viewpoint is the pretribulation rapture, a view which is unacceptable to those who think the Church will be raptured at the middle of the tribulation period and to those who think the Church will go through the tribulation.

One fact, which admits of no contradiction, in the midst of a rich variety of viewpoints, is that Jesus is coming again to this earth. The Apostles' Creed, for example, says that Jesus is "seated at the right hand of God the Father from whence He shall come to judge the quick and the dead." The great creeds of the Church have always affirmed the same truth. Jesus is coming again. This affirmation is consistent with, and thoroughly embedded in, the Scriptures. Moreover, from the philosophical perspective, if history had a beginning as it did in the Garden of Eden in the persons of Adam and Eve, so must it also have an end or consummation. If history began with the paradise which was lost because of Adam's sin, so must it also have a paradise regained. If the history of redemption had a beginning, so must there be its final fulfillment.

In a still larger context, the second advent of Jesus Christ is related to what might be called "the invisible war." The history of the redemption of the planet Earth constitutes only a portion, however large or small it may be, of the cosmic struggle being waged throughout the whole universe. This struggle has for its chief protagonists God and Satan. This battle between good and evil has for its objective the sovereign control of the universe either by God the creator or Satan the usurper. One or the other will emerge victorious.

So far as the visible aspect of the war is concerned, the earth is the focal point of the warfare. It was to this planet Earth God sent his only begotten Son. It was on a cross outside the city gates of Jerusalem on the brow of a hill called Calvary that the Son of the living God was crucified. It was at the cross that the righteousness of God was vindicated by Christ's atoning death. His sacrifice made possible the redemption of sinful men. By his death he opened the gates of heaven through which all those who receive him by faith enter its portals, having been reconciled to God. But there is more to the story than that.

The act which made possible the salvation of men also brought about the defeat of Satan. The archenemy of God who fought to supplant the Creator and to wrest his throne from him was dealt a death blow. Satan, in the form of a serpent, bruised the heel of the Messiah at Calvary. But the Redeemer dealt the Serpent a crushing blow to his head at the cross. Satan, then, is already defeated. Christ's victory over him has been firmly established in principle.

But the wounded Serpent in his death throes continues to writhe and lash out at God and men. His power has not yet been finally extinguished and will not be until death and hell overtake him. Although he continues to exude his venom, the changeless plan and triumphant will of God are being perfectly fulfilled among men and throughout the universe. Satan, God's enemy, has a vast army under his control and command. That army includes hordes of demons who joined Satan in his original rebellion against the Creator. It includes, on this earth, the hordes of men who have allied themselves with Satan against God in their own efforts to usurp his sovereignty and defeat his purposes. Their malignity is expressed in many forms, not the least of which is to pose as friends of God when they are counterfeits. They are really God's enemies, and whoever is the enemy of God is the enemy of the Church and of all the saints of God.

Jesus, whose final victory will come to pass when he returns to this earth, could not come again in glory and great power had he not come the first time in the form of a servant, fashioned after the likeness of sinful flesh. His first advent was prophetically foretold by the ancient prophets, who spelled out specifically many things concerning his person and program. He was to come from Abraham's loins through Isaac, Jacob, Judah, David, and the Virgin Mary. The time of his coming was announced by the prophet Daniel. The wise men brought tidings to Herod of the birth of the king. The natal sign was the "star in the east" which troubled Herod and all Jerusalem and led to the inquiry concerning the words of the prophets.

King Herod gathered the chief priests and the scribes in Jerusalem and demanded of them where the Christ child should be born. They did not dissent from the testimony of the wise men as to the time of Jesus' coming, and they bore witness to the prophet's word that Bethlehem was the site of the birth of the expected Messiah.

Herod's worst fears of a competitor for his royal throne were aroused. In his fury he slaughtered all of the male innocents of Bethlehem two years of age and under. But Mary and Joseph, led by the Spirit of God, fled to Egypt for a season until Herod's death at which time they returned.

One major mystery connected with Jesus' first advent remains forever to perplex us, for its implications have a bearing on his second advent as well. The time of Jesus' first advent was unchangeably fixed, according to the prophecy of the seventy weeks in the Book of Daniel (chapter 9). Each week was reckoned as seven years. The seventy weeks represented a period of 490 years. The first seven weeks or forty-nine years was the period marked by the "commandment to restore and rebuild Jerusalem." This command was given by Artaxerxes between 454 and 444 B.C. When the sixty-two weeks or 434 years are added, it brings us to the time of Christ. When the sixty-nine weeks or 483 years ended, it meant that no one could thereafter claim to be the Messiah according to Scripture. Thus, no one born today could be the Messiah, nor could anyone who was born since that time nearly two thousand years ago.

Since the time of the Savior's birth was fixed by prophetic Scripture, it seems strange indeed that the scribes and teachers of Israel did not recognize and accept Jesus as the promised One. This is especially true for two reasons. First, no man spoke as Jesus spoke. This the Jewish leaders had to admit. At the tender age of twelve, Jesus confounded the teachers of the law with his knowledge and discernment. But Jesus added the witness of his works to the witness of his words. When John the Baptist in the despondency of his imprisonment sent two of his disciples to Jesus, they asked the Master this question: "Art thou he that should come, or do we look for another?" Jesus told them to return to John and to report "those things which ye do hear and see" (Matt. 11:3, 4). His words were supported by his works—the deaf talked, the lame walked, the sick were healed, and the dead were raised. Thus the Scribes and Pharisees were twofold children of hell for they neither believed his words nor his works.

John recorded another instance when Jesus said: "though ye believe not me, believe the works: that ye may know, and believe, that the Father is in me, and I in him" (John 10:38). They responded by attempting to seize him and kill him "but he escaped out of their hand" (John 10:39).

The lamentable folly of the Jews is plain. They denied the witness of the Old Testament to the first coming of their Messiah. They denied the words of Jesus himself when he did come. And they denied his works, which were the credentials of his messiahship. The climax of the folly of Jewish leadership came when they brought about his crucifixion, rejoicing in his death.

May we not say that in the first advent of Jesus, Satan in some measure did gain an advantage? He did blind the eyes of many to what should have been plain to them. But Satan's deception would have had no effect had the Jews of Jesus' day sided with God rather than with Satan in the invisible war for control of the universe.

The same Scriptures which speak of Jesus' first advent also speak about his second coming. Among those who are called Christians there are some who laugh at the doctrine of the second advent. They are pawns in the hands of Satan. They commit the same sin that so many of the Jews in Jesus' day committed. They do not believe the words of the prophets, the apostles, and the Lord Jesus. The problem does not consist in the want of words affirming the second coming. Rather it lies in the lack of confidence in the words which speak of that coming. No solution to this problem exists once Scripture is overlooked or repudiated, for man has no other way to know that there is a second advent or, for that matter, that history has a consummation. The sentence in the Apostles' Creed "from thence He shall come to judge the quick and the dead" did not spring from the minds of men. It is firmly rooted in the revelation of God found only in the Bible. Thus if the Scriptures are not dependable, the notion of Jesus' second advent has no warrant and is not worthy of credence.

The foundation on which our discussion rests is the belief in the second advent of Jesus, which finds its warrant in Scripture. For this reason the only question which can be asked is, Does the Bible teach the second coming of our Lord? If the answer is in the negative, nothing more needs to be said apart from mere speculation. But if the response is yes, then other questions come to the fore which require a great deal of discussion. This may be illustrated from Jesus' first coming. Once it is accepted that there was a first advent, then one can ask correctly: When would it take place? What would its purpose be? What signs would alert and inform men as they waited for that advent? What would enable them to recognize the true Messiah when he did make his appearance?

Humanly speaking, from the vantage point of the first advent of Jesus, the most conclusive evidence of his uniqueness and messiahship lies in his bodily resurrection from the dead. The virgin birth admits of no human evidence apart from the witness and testimony of Mary and Joseph. Christ's death on Calvary to the onlooker did nothing more than testify to the multitudes that a man named Jesus of Nazareth died there. Its ultimate meaning cannot be certified by human inquiry and makes no sense unless one accepts what has been revealed by God himself.

The resurrection, however, is quite different. It was a historical event, open to the sense perceptions of multitudes of believers. They saw the one who had been embalmed and placed in the tomb and now had risen from the dead. They perceived his wounds. They ate with him. They listened to his teaching for forty days. They watched him as he ascended into the heavens. The empty tomb ever stands as a rebuke to faithless men who try to explain away the unexplainable by substituting silly theories—a stolen body, a visit to the wrong tomb, the later death of a decrepit and dying Jesus, and hallucinations suffered by multitudes who believed what wasn't true and whose fevered imaginations were deceived for forty days and nights.

The claim that the bodily resurrection of Jesus is invalidated because he was seen only by his disciples and not by men of unbelief carries no weight. The demand of unbelievers that God's plan and program, his agenda, should or must be set up by them would subject God to the whims of men. This cannot be. God's ways are not the ways of men. Men can and do reject what God has done but they are reactors, not originators, of what God determines and does. Moreover, the testimony of those who were most intimate with Jesus and who were numbered among his followers carries far greater weight than the perverse ramblings of those who could not see the forest because of the trees. This much is plain. A dead Jesus could not come again; only a living one can do this.

Having asserted that Jesus is coming the second time, we can go on from there to address the many and varied questions which flow from this conviction. These questions are similar to those which devout believers in the Old Testament asked about the first coming of Jesus: When will it take place? Why has he delayed so long in coming? What will the purpose of that coming be? What are the signs of this approaching event? How do we fit Israel and the Church into the divine scheme of things? Both comings of Jesus are related to history and of this a word should be said.

History has to do with the known and unknown. The known in history can be quite deceptive, however, unless there is some manner by which the unknown can be ascertained and related to the known. Illustrations of this puzzler abound. A famous case in American history relates to Judge Crater from New York City. One day he disappeared from sight. That's all we know. Whether he committed suicide, was murdered, or is alive and sheltered from public view we do not know. The unknown in this case is important.

Take the case of a man who deserts his wife. She never hears from him again. All we know is that he has deserted her, leaving behind a note to that effect. The reason or reasons for his conduct are left to the imagination. Until the true reasons become available, the unknown is greater than the known and the history is incomplete.

Looking at history from the Christian or biblical perspective, we can say that there are two kinds of history: the secular or profane and the sacred. Secular history does have its puzzles, but philosophically we may say that it is the record of man's doings, with God left out of the picture. The very notion of a God who is active in history runs counter to the thought patterns of the secular man, whether Marxist or humanist. God in history starts with the supernatural. The secular mind thinks in terms of the natural, however, and thus excludes God from the historical processes. When the supernatural is omitted, then events like the virgin birth, the substitutionary atonement of Jesus, his bodily resurrection from the dead, and his second coming are looked upon askance and thrown into the waste heap. They constitute non-events or religious superstitions.

Christian revelation begins with the presupposition that all history is sacred history. Indeed there is secular history which we can probe into and write about. But behind all secular history God is at work and is in control of the levers of history. As the Lord of history, God has his own plan in operation, unknown to those who disregard the Bible. Yet the divine plan or cosmic purpose is being carried out inexorably because God is sovereign. The hidden strand or sacred aspect of history can be known to men, believers and unbelievers, only when God chooses to disclose what he is doing behind the scenes and how his purposes are being fulfilled.

A casual statement by Golda Meir, onetime prime minister of Israel, illustrates the point. She made reference to Moses, the human founder of the nation Israel and its great lawgiver. "Moses wasn't so smart," she said. "He brought the Israelites into Palestine and it's the only land in the Near East which has no oil." Now that's quite true. But the God who put the oil in the earth knew quite well what he was doing. An oilless Israel is essential to the outworking purpose of God in relation to Jesus' second coming.

Moreover, God is in control of all the nations of the world. It is no accident that communists control a large portion of the globe and are moving forward aggressively to take over more nations and peoples. The fact that communism is autocratic and inhuman, and that its socialism cannot and will not solve humankind's problems is beside the point. As we shall see, the communists will play a decisive role in bringing about the consummation of history. What the communist powers are doing so far as sacred history is concerned is unknown to them; they are fulfilling the larger plan of God which will result in their undoing at last.

Of course, Christians should oppose communism with all their might as part of their struggle against evil and for the rights of all men. When they have done all they can to stem the tide, if God allows communism to prevail in numerous parts of the western world, they must accept it as within the will of God even as they continue their opposition to it.

God indeed can bring down a democracy and socialize a productive, free-enterprise economy. When it does occur, rarely is it perceived as springing from the directive will of God, for superficially, greater wrong seems to have triumphed over what at its worst is a lesser evil. Moreover, when this happens, the consent and machinations of strategic elements within the conquered nation make its overthrow possible. Sometimes do-good, professing Christians, realizing the evils of an economic system in which men have forgotten their stewardship role, embrace idealistically the notion of a society in which all men will be brothers and where wealth will be distributed on the basis "from each according to his ability, to each according to his need." But in every instance a worse form of evil has replaced a lesser one, and men lose the freedom they formerly enjoyed. Alexander Solzhenitsyn has repeatedly emphasized the point that the idealist vision is a myth which becomes a human nightmare when socialism becomes a reality. The Christian, however, knows that all events, even those which have in them the greatest potential for evil, remain within the sovereign control of God and cannot come about unless God allows them to do so.

One grand illustration of the outworking of God in history is apparent in the first advent of Jesus. God brought to pass three circumstances essential to the divine purpose in sending Jesus. There was a universal language—the koine Greek tongue. It was spoken everywhere in the ancient world of that day. The New Testament was in fact written in that universal tongue.

Secondly, there was universal peace (the pax Romana) which existed at the birth of Christ. The Temple of Janus, which remained open whenever there was war, was closed for the first time in several centuries. The Roman republic had given way to the emperorship, and the troops of Caesar Augustus were stationed all around the mighty empire as keepers of the peace in a stabilized and prosperous world.

Thirdly, the Romans had built the greatest system of roads the world had ever known. These roads circled the empire. The pax Romana guaranteed safety, and the roads made travel possible on a scale hitherto unknown among men. The Apostle Paul was able to use these roads to bring the gospel to all the people in the Mediterranean basin. God did use the pagan empire of Rome to bring to pass what was part of the divine plan for the evangelization of the world.

What was true at the time of the birth of Christ was also generally true in the Old Testament. God was in control of all the nations and used them to fulfill his purposes. God used the rulers of the people with whom Abraham came into contact to protect him. God prospered his great-grandson, Joseph, in Egypt and through him the children of Jacob found a place where they could become a multitude in safety. The bondage they endured in Egypt became the motivation for their deliverance from Pharaoh, a deliverance arranged by God as part of sacred history which included the miracles of Moses and the crossing of the Red Sea dryshod.

The nations who occupied Palestine had reached the point of no return. God used the Israelites to execute divine judgment on peoples whose iniquities were unrestrained and who refused to repent and turn to God in faith. Faithless and unbelieving men find it difficult to accept the fact that God ordered the extermination of the Canaanites even as they have failed to see that their continued presence in the land would have been a constant invitation to Israel to apostatize.

Before the Exodus took place, God told Moses that he would harden Pharaoh's heart (Exod. 4:21). God even said to Moses: "See, I have made thee a god to Pharaoh" (Exod. 7:1). And, "I will harden Pharaoh's heart" (Exod. 7:3). "And he [God] hardened Pharoah's heart, that he hearkened not unto them; as the Lord had said" (Exod. 7:13). Once the children of Israel escaped from Egypt, Jethro, Moses' father-in-law, brought Zipporah along with Gershom and Eliezer to Moses in the wilderness. "And Moses told his father-in-law all that the Lord had done unto Pharaoh and to the Egyptians for Israel's sake" (Exod. 18:8). The secular historian, of course, could note what had happened. But he would never attribute the responsibility for what happened to God and sacred history. The most that any secular historian would say is that Moses *thought* God was working through him without admitting the reality of the idea.

When the children of Israel fought against Amalek and prevailed, the reason for the victory was that Aaron and Hur held up Moses' hands. As long as his hands were held up, the Israelites prevailed and slaughtered the enemy. Moses' upheld hands were instrumental in the victory but the secular historian can only laugh at this aspect of the affair.

Samson was one of Israel's judges. His father and mother remonstrated with him when he wished to marry a Philistine girl. What Samson's parents did not understand was that God, in sacred history, was at work. So the Scripture says: "his father and mother knew not that it was of the Lord, that he sought an occasion against the Philistines" (Judg. 14:4).

God's control of the nations can be seen also in the writings of the Old Testament prophets. Secular and sacred history are so conjoined that they demonstrate with the greatest clarity that secular history is dominated and controlled by sacred history. Thus great nations rose and fell, and rise and fall today, according to God's sovereign good pleasure. God so works that secular historians do not perceive his operations. In their writings these historians give their readers no hints that God's edicts are involved in the historical movements they depict. The historians themselves write with the conviction that if there is a God he is remote so that nations determine their own destinies. Whatever happens is the consequence of man's activities, for no power operating behind the outward situations is regarded as possible by the historians.

Mighty Babylon of yesteryear was the largest superpower and mightiest conqueror of its day. Yet this empire fell. But no secular textbook of history attributes its fall to the will and the plan of God. It was Jeremiah the prophet who wrote what the secular historians have refused to say. This is his perception of Babylon's fall:

> Thus saith the Lord; Behold I will raise up against Babylon, and against them that dwell in the midst of them that rise up against me, a destroying wind; And will send unto Babylon fanners, that shall fan her, and shall empty her land . . . Babylon is suddenly fallen and destroyed. . . . The Lord hath raised up the spirit of the kings of the Medes: for his device is against Babylon to destroy it; because it is the vengeance of the Lord . . . . And Babylon shall become heaps, a dwellingplace for dragons, an

astonishment, and an hissing, without an inhabitant [Jer. 51:1, 2, 8, 11, 37].

Exekiel wrote about that which has not yet happened but which would surely come to pass in the not too distant future. He said:

> And the word of the Lord came unto me, saying, Son of man, set thy face against Gog, the land of Magog, the chief prince of Meshech and Tubal, and prophesy against him, And say, Thus saith the Lord God; Behold I am against thee, O Gog, the chief prince of Meshech and Tubal: And I will turn thee back, and put hooks into thy jaws, and I will bring thee forth, and all thine army, horses and horsemen, all of them clothed with all sorts of armour, even a great company with bucklers and shields, all of them handling swords [Ezek. 38:1-4].

This is Almighty God at work in the history of men.

Amos stated clearly that the fall of many nations was the direct consequence of the divine fiat of God. He wrote about Damascus:

> Thus saith the Lord; For three transgressions of Damascus, and for four, I will not turn away the punishment thereof; because they have threshed Gilead with threshing instruments of iron: But I will send a fire into the house of Hazael, which shall devour the palaces of Benhadad. I will break also the bar of Damascus, and cut off the inhabitant from the plain of Aven, and him that holdeth the sceptre from the house of Eden: and the people of Syria shall go into captivity unto Kir, saith the Lord [Amos 1:3-5].

Of Gaza, Amos said:

> Thus saith the Lord; For three transgressions of Gaza, and for four, I will not turn away the punishment thereof; because they carried away captive the whole captivity, to deliver them up to Edom: But I will send a fire on the wall of Gaza, which shall devour the palaces thereof [Amos 1:6, 7].

Amos attributed the fall of Tyre to God:

> Thus saith the Lord; For three transgressions of Tyrus, and for four, I will not turn away the punishment thereof;

because they delivered up the whole captivity to Edom,
and remembered not the brotherly covenant: But I will
send a fire on the walls of Tyrus, which will devour the
palaces thereof [Amos 1:9, 10].

Of Edom, Amos bespoke the consuming judgment of God:
Thus saith the Lord; for three transgressions of Edom,
and for four, I will not turn away the punishment thereof; because he did pursue his brother with the sword, and
did cast off all pity, and his anger did tear perpetually,
and he kept his wrath for ever. But I will send a fire upon
Teman, which shall devour the palaces of Bozrah [Amos
1:11, 12].

Scripture clearly affirms that God is not the God of benign
neglect. He does not allow the nations (any nation) to go their
own ways, nor does he permit them to do anything which
would annul, undercut, or subvert the divine plan for the consummation of history. The long passage of history and the fact
that God's interposition in the affairs of men are often hidden
from human sight are not to be taken as disinterest or abdica-
tion by him. His ways are not our ways, and a day is as a thousand years and a thousand years as a day.

The worst mistake that can be made is to conclude that if God
was active in history in former ages he is not active today. He
is no less active at this moment than he was when he formed
and fashioned the universe. Thus the rise of communism must
be understood within the context of God's larger plan. The
current emergence of the Soviet Union as one of the two most
powerful nations in the world is no accident of history. It is
part of the divine purpose.

If the Christian understanding of the past must include God
as the God of history, it is no less important for us to include
him in the events of today, which point inexorably and certainly to the second coming of Jesus Christ as King of kings and
Lord of lords. One point, of transcendent significance with
respect to God as the God of history, remains to be made.

God the Creator owns all of his creation. He has title to all the
lands of the planet Earth. He allocates lands to whomever he
pleases and in accord with his unvarying purpose. Land is
loaned to men and nations but the title to the land ever re-

mains in the hands of God. This is important as we consider the gathering storm and the events which will precede the coming of the Lord.

As we shall see, the land of Palestine is designed by God to be the centerpiece of the events surrounding the end times. Today two currently opposing parties are laying claim to Palestine: the Jews and the Arabs. Both parties at one time or another have occupied this land. But there have been times when it was occupied by neither Jews nor Arabs. The right to possession or eminent domain is derived from certain conditions, according to nonsacred history. In the long history of man, title can derive from conquest. The empires of ancient history accepted this right based on force. In modern history the British Empire was created by conquest. Until recently it was the largest empire in modern history and it could rightfully claim that the sun never set on it. The French, Spanish, and Portuguese empires were established by force. Today the empire of the Soviet Union is based on force and conquest. Its subject peoples have no means to redress their servitude.

The right to possession can also be based on occupation of the land or living on the land over an extended period of time. In America we call it squatter's rights. Certainly the Arab claim to Palestine is based upon their living in, and their control of, the land for many centuries. The Jews, of course, lay claim to the land because they occupied it before the Arabs did. When Israel was recognized as a nation in 1948 by the United Nations it was given sovereignty over a small portion of Palestine. The unsuccessful Arab efforts to dislodge the Israelis by war and their consequent defeat only enabled the Israelis to increase their land holdings by conquest. Thus the Israeli claim to what they now occupy is partly based on military conquest, a long standing basis for nations to claim possession.

When we look at Palestine from the standpoint of sacred history a somewhat different perspective emerges. Scripture distinguishes between possession and ownership. The ownership of land, and all other things as well, belongs ultimately to God who lends these things to men as a stewardship. No man or nation, humanly speaking, has a right to take from other men what God has loaned or given title to. To take what belongs to others who have received it as a gift from God is stealing, and stealing is prohibited. But a sovereign God can and does transfer possession of land from one people to another. Since possession constitutes title, the title can be abrogated only by God himself who is the ultimate owner of all.

God in history sovereignly allocated Palestine to his people Israel. This piece of land is at best only a tiny fragment of this planet, yet it has a strategic significance light years more important than its size. In the drama of redemption and in the unseen war between God and Satan, Palestine is the focal point of reference. It was here that Jesus became flesh. It was here that he lived, spoke, died, and rose again. It was here that he left our planet and it is here he will return in power and glory. Jerusalem will someday be the center of the world. Nehemiah recorded how God chose Abraham and spoke of the covenant he made with him:

> Thou art the Lord the God, who didst choose Abram, and broughtest him forth out of Ur of the Chaldees, and gavest him the name of Abraham; And foundest his heart faithful before thee, and madest a covenant with him to give the land of the Canaanites, the Hittites, the Amorites, and the Perizzites, and the Jebusites, and the Girgashites, to give it, I say, to his seed, and hast performed thy words; for thou art righteous [Neh. 9:7, 8].

God dispossessed the Canaanites, the Hittites, the Amorites, the Perizzites, the Jebusites and the Girgashites. He gave their lands to Israel forever. But the *forever* must be qualified, since a lapse would take place between the time Israel would be temporarily dispossessed from the land and when the land would become Israel's in perpetuity. God's everlasting covenant with Abraham was conditioned in time, although not in eternity, by one reservation: Israel's obedience to God.

Moses in Deuteronomy 28 spelled out the consequences flowing from Israel's obedience or disobedience. Beginning with verse sixty-two, the awful results of disobedience are made plain. God would scatter his people among the nations. They would fear for their lives night and day. Disobedience would delay, not annul, God's covenant promise. A day would come when Israel would obey God from the heart and Palestine would be Israel's forever.

Israel's first punishment for disobedience was the destruction of the Northern Kingdom in 722-721 B.C. The second major judgment was the Babylonian Captivity of the Southern Kingdom in 586 B.C. when God used Nebuchadnezzar as his agent of destruction. The throne of David was vacant, waiting for that day when Messiah King, Jesus Christ, would sit on the throne of his father David to order and establish it forever. When Jesus arrived on the scene, the Jews spurned him as Messiah. The full measure of divine wrath was visited upon a faithless people: Jerusalem was destroyed by the legions of Vespasian and Titus in A.D. 70. The city came under the control of the Gentiles from that time forward and the Jews were dispersed among the nations of the world. Palestine was no longer under the control of the Jews and the Jewish kingdom in any form disappeared from the face of the earth to await a recovery of the kingdom under David's greater son at a later date.

The conclusion of the matter is this. God is the God of history. He is fully in control of all things. Thus profane or secular history is flawed by the refusal to include God or sacred history in the affairs of men. This refusal derives from the unregenerate condition of secular man in which estate man is the end of all things. In his own inimitable way, Alexander Solzhenitsyn has written:

> . . . all of us are standing on the brink of a great historical cataclysm, a flood that swallows up civilization and changes whole epochs. The present world situation is complicated still more by the fact that several hours have struck simultaneously on the clock of history. We all must face up to a crisis—not just a social crisis, not just a political crisis, not just a military crisis—face up to it, but all to stand firm in this great upheaval, an upheaval similar to that which marked the transition from the Middle Ages to the Renaissance. Just as mankind once became aware of the intolerable and mistaken deviations of the Middle Ages and recoiled in horror from it, so too must we take account of the disastrous deviation of the late Enlightenment. We have become hopelessly enmeshed in our slavish worship of all that is pleasant, all that is comfortable, all that is material—we worship things, we worship products.

Will we ever succeed in shaking off this burden in giving free rein to the spirit that was breathed into us at birth, that spirit which distinguishes us from the animal world? [*Warning to the West,* (New York: Farrar, Straus, and Giroux, 1976), pp. 145, 146.]

What then is the answer to Alexander Solzhenitsyn's questions? There can be no doubt that an upheaval is upon us which is shaking the nations. But will it lead to a new age of human history? No, indeed. Sacred history tells us differently. The end of the age is coming upon us. The climax of history will soon take place. The second advent of Christ, the Lord of history, is imminent. That which some of God's people have proclaimed boldly, prayed for fervently, and waited for patiently for almost two thousand years will take place in the not-too-distant future.

The time is at hand even if we do not know and cannot know the exact day or the hour. The Lord of history is about to finish the work he began in Eden when Adam first sinned. He is about to end the dominance of the prince of this world who has always led men astray. God has given us signs for the times, signs which signal to faithful students of Scripture the soon coming of Christ in power and glory. How do we know this, and what are the reasons for believing this with any certainty? What follows now are the answers to these questions. Contemporary events, in ways never before known, foreshadow Christ's soon coming. In a day when men say, "Peace, peace," they will find no peace, and sudden destruction comes. No new secular age of worldwide peace is coming. Instead there will be the *gathering storm* which will lead shortly to Armageddon.

Before stating how contemporary events signal the soon coming of Christ, some attention must be paid to the different views of that coming entertained by Christians across the centuries. In bygone generations, perhaps the most widely held view was the postmillennial one. It is no longer a popular view for a number of good reasons.

Perhaps it was Augustine through his writings who popularized postmillennialism more than anyone else. In his great book *The City of God,* he expected the kingdom of God to grow in history until it filled the whole earth. When the Christian faith had penetrated the world, a glorious thousand year age would dawn among men and righteousness would prevail on earth. At the end of the glorious age, Christ would return and the final judgment would take place after the resurrection of the righteous and unrighteous dead. Time would come to an end and eternity would begin.

In America, postmillennialism was popular in orthodox circles in the nineteenth and early twentieth centuries. Among theological liberals, optimism abounded following World War I and the advent of a utopian society was thought to be imminent. The Paris Peace Pact of 1928 was hailed as the harbinger of the new age when war would be no more. The worldwide depression, the rise of Nazi Germany, the emergence of the Soviet Union as a world power, and World War II with the genocide of the Jews, cut through that rosy optimism. Under Stalin, even liberals like Reinhold Niebuhr experienced a turnabout and talked about the rampant demonism in men and society. Liberal optimism was succeeded by neoorthodoxy with its more balanced view of sin.

Among the theological orthodox in the nineteenth century the famed theologian, Charles Hodge, was a postmillenialist. When postmillennialism died to all practical intents and purposes, it was replaced by premillennialism among some who had formerly been postmillennialists. Most of the postmillennialists became amillennialists. Among evangelicals there are still a few postmillennalists, but they are by no means a significant company either in numbers or in influence.

Curiously enough, communism has a utopian aspect about it, but its very utopian view of man is negated by the failure of communism to produce a single perfect human being as well as by communism's sorry record of murder by the millions among those whom they term bourgeoisie. The communist movement has brought more people under its aegis than any empire or movement in man's history. Its proclaimed promise is worldwide peace and harmony brought about, strangely enough, by force. Needless to say, a peace brought into being by the murder of the opposition, and the proclamation of communism's new man who does not exist anywhere gives the lie to the propaganda. What is oddest of all is the fact that liberal churchmen of the twenties, who thought the world had beaten its swords into plowshares and its spears into pruning hooks, have raised a new generation of like-minded Bible-denying followers who have swallowed the communist propaganda, hook, line, and sinker. They now pound the drums for the use of force to do away with injustice in their fight against what they and the communists call the imperialists of the west.

Nowhere is the ecclesiastical encouragement of revolution and terrorism more explicitly demonstrated than in the World Council of Churches. This body has in its membership an overwhelming number of protestant and orthodox bodies (exclusive of the Roman Catholic Church and a few large bodies like the Southern Baptist Convention). The London *Daily Telegram* (Nov. 5, 1979) ran a piece about the World Council of Churches. The author, Canon D. W. Grundy, noted that "Church of England dioceses are being asked to contribute £100,000 over the next seven years to the community and race relations unit of the council, which makes grants to unspecified projects, including the Marxist Race Today Collective."

One Church of England spokesman said: "The way the communist ideology is taking over the 'whole' mind of the Anglican Church is truly disastrous. So far few of the laity seem either willing or able to resist." The Rev. Christopher Wansey, "former member of the General Synod" strongly condemned "the averred humanitarian aid to so-called 'liberation movements.' He said: "On the facts as I see them, these organizations are 'terrorist groups.' " And so they are. Clearly the ecumenical movement is seeking to bring in the kingdom by force and the support, financially and ideologically, of the communist viewpoint. Liberalism's man-oriented program to bring about a peaceful world is now a program based on terrorism and military or revolutionary force.

Postmillennialism appears to be a dead option to most Bible-believing people in this generation. The facts of history lend it no support and biblical hermeneutics must be bent if a case is to be made for it. This brings us to the second eschatological option, amillennialism.

Amillennialism differs from premillennialism and postmillennialism in one important regard. It does not think there will be a thousand-year reign of peace on earth either before or after the coming of the Lord. This present age will come to its close when Christ returns. At that time there will be a general resurrection of the dead followed by the judgment, at which time eternity will begin.

By and large, amillennialism does not look for the literal fulfillment of the Old Testament prophecies concerning Israel. Rather, the Church is thought to be the new Israel. It does not anticipate the construction of a temple on Mount Zion, nor does it find place in history for the regathering of Israel to Palestine from the four corners of the earth. Moreover, amillennialism has never held to a secret, any-moment rapture of the Church and it does not anticipate any pretribulational or mid-tribulational rapture either. It does expect the worsening of world conditions and regards the Pauline warning about the characteristics of the closing days of this age seriously.

Some amillennialists are disappointed postmillennialists who cannot embrace a literal fulfillment of the Old Testament prophecies with respect to Israel. This standpoint de-historicizes many of the Old Testament prophetic Scriptures and introduces a hermeneutic distinctly different from that of the premillennialist. This does not mean that amillennialists are theological liberals, although there may be some who are. Most of them are in agreement with premillennialists that Christ is coming personally, and visibly, and in mighty power.

Eschatological differences at this point should not be interpreted as a betrayal of historic orthodoxy. Rather, eschatology should be looked upon as susceptible to differing understandings similar to differences among Christian brethren about water baptism, church polity, and the nature of the elements served at the communion table. To take this stance does not mean that one's view about the second coming of Jesus Christ is marginal or unimportant. If the premillennialist is right, then the other views are incorrect. But we do see through a glass darkly and should be able to discuss the issue without rancor.

It is interesting to note in this connection that premillennialists almost to a man are part of the fundamentalist or evangelical movements. They take Scripture very seriously and very few premillennialists would deny biblical inerrancy.

Those most active in evangelism and missions are premillennialists. The Interdenominational Foreign Mission Association, which has in its membership some eight thousand missionaries, has a premillennial plank in its doctrinal platform. Virtually all Bible colleges and Bible churches are premillennial. Evangelical colleges like Wheaton and Westmont are, too. Billy Graham, Bill Bright, Jerry Falwell, and Richard DeHaan are premillennialists. So is the Moody Bible Institute and so are a multitude of the religious broadcasting stations around the globe. Premillennialism is, then, the third option over against postmillennialism and amillennialism.

A substantial number of premillennialists are committed to dispensational theology. This viewpoint is quite specific about the order of events for the closing days of this age. Perhaps the Scofield Bible has been the most influential force in teaching dispensationalism for nearly a century. The new Scofield Bible has altered some of Dr. Scofield's conclusions and of this more will be said later. In the meantime, as Scofield described the eschatology of dispensational adherents, the following points should be emphasized.

Scofield distinguished sharply between Israel and the Church. According to Scofield's view, the latter is said to be a mystery not made known in the Old Testament. Israel and the Church are looked upon as two distinct entities with two different destinies. The Church age is regarded as a parenthesis which began at Pentecost and will end when the Church is raptured before the period known as the tribulation begins. The people (Jews and Gentiles alike) saved during the tribulation period are not thought to be part of the Church. Salvation will come to many of the Jews who will turn to Christ and who will finish the work of world evangelization. The Holy Spirit will be "taken out of the way" when the Church is raptured. Scofield says that this is "the removal of that which restrains the mystery of lawlessness" (p. 1272).

Moreover Dr. Scofield said that seven signs are to precede the day of the Lord: (1) the sending of Elijah; (2) cosmical disturbances; (3) the insensibility of the professing church; (4) the apostasy of the professing church, then become "Laodicea"; (5) the rapture of the true church; (6) the manifestation of "the man of sin"; (7) the apocalyptic judgments (p. 1349). Of this and other aspects of Dr. Scofield's teaching more will be said later.

It is important to remember in discussing the matter that the central key to the understanding of the differences between dispensational and nondispensational premillennialism seems to center around the pretribulational rapture of the Church. I have seen no writings of dispensationalists who are not pretribulational rapturists. It is fair to say that, historically, pretribulational dispensationalism is of recent origin. The more important question is not whether it has a long history but whether it is hermeneutically correct. It is also fair to say that what we call historical premillennialism has generally held to a posttribulational rapture of the Church.

I do not know of any premillennialists who deny that the Church will be raptured. The real question is when the rapture will occur. This will be discussed in detail later, after the main point of the book has been explored. So we turn our attention to the question: What are the contemporary events which convincingly indicate that we are either close to, or in, the closing days of this age?

2

ISRAEL A SIGN OF CHRIST'S SOON COMING

ISRAEL IS ONE OF THE KEYS TO THE END OF THE AGE. Whoever loses sight of Israel and its role in the events connected with the consummation of history has an incorrect view of the second advent of Jesus. It cannot be otherwise. It would be most inappropriate to suppose that God, who used Israel to bring the Church age into being, is finished with the people who go by that name and that he has no more interest in them. The Christian faith is truly the Judeo-Christian faith. We have the Old Testament as well as the New Testament. It is true that we understand the Old Testament by what is contained in the New Testament. But that is so because God's revelation is progressive. Thus there are segments of the Christian faith which are more fully explicated and made plainer in the New Testament.

The Christian faith of the New Testament is rooted and grounded in the Old Testament. Paul and James looked back to Father Abraham and told us that we are children of Abraham by faith. He is the original progenitor of our tradition. He is one from whom the priesthood (Levi) and the kingship (Judah) sprang through his grandson Jacob. Jesus is a descendant of Abraham, Jacob, Judah, and David. Jesus is a Jew, an Israelite. It was Jesus who said, "Your father Abraham rejoiced to see my day: and he saw it, and was glad" (John 8:56). This Jesus was the Lamb of God slain from before the foundation of the world. God knew from the beginning that Jesus would atone for our sins. And somehow Abraham knew this too. We cannot fully understand all that is contained in the statement of Jesus about Abraham but, in some fashion not fully known to us yet, Abraham knew of the coming of the Messiah and of his atoning death by the same kind of saving faith we have as we look back to Calvary.

Abraham was the founding father of the nation Israel, too. From his loins came the people who were delivered from their bondage in Egypt. This Egyptian experience is popularly mis-understood today, especially by those who are enamoured by the theology of liberation. They use the Israeli experience as a prototype for liberation from economic, social, and political oppression. In so doing, they miss one main point. God sent his people into Egypt, not as a punishment for their sins, but as a place where they could grow and become a great nation. When they had reached this point, their very size was a threat to the Egyptians, and God used that as a reason for delivering them from Egypt so they might occupy the land of Palestine which he had promised to Abraham and his descendants. In all of this, God was the deliverer, not man.

It was under Moses that God laid before the people of Israel the terms of his covenant which was conditioned upon their obedience. Israel was a theocracy with God as the king. The Book of Deuteronomy contains some of the most important details having to do with the plan of God for the ages. Rational critics have said this book was composed in the sixth century B.C. Conservative scholars have always agreed that the book was written by Moses and was not a mishmash put together centuries after the events. Deuteronomy 28 lays before Israel, in the clearest fashion, the terms the nation must fulfill if the blessing of God is to follow them. The chapter opens with a verse containing the word "if." "*If* thou shalt hearken diligently unto the voice of the Lord thy God, to observe and to do all his commandments which I command thee this day . . . all these blessings shall come on thee, and overtake thee, *if* thou shalt hearken unto the voice of the Lord thy God" (28:1, 2, italics mine). And Moses enumerated the blessings which follow obedience, blessings anyone in his right mind would desire to have.

When Moses finished enumerating the blessings for obedience, the Holy Spirit laid down the consequences which would follow disobedience. It is sad indeed to suppose that any people would disobey God after he had spelled out the glorious promises of blessing for obedience. But God knew the hearts of the people of Israel, hearts that were no different from the hearts of many people today. He left them without excuse, so that they could never be able to justify themselves by saying that God had not warned them what the consequences of disobedience would be. The most awful segment of chapter 28 is contained in verses 63 to 67.

> And it shall come to pass, that as the Lord rejoiced over you to do you good, and to multiply you; so the Lord will rejoice over you to destroy you, and to bring you to nought; and ye shall be plucked from off the land whither thou goest to possess it. And the Lord shall scatter thee among all people, from the one end of the earth even unto the other; and there thou shalt serve other gods, which neither thou nor thy fathers have known, even wood and stone. And among these nations shalt thou find no ease, neither shall the sole of thy foot have rest: but the Lord shall give thee there a trembling heart, and failing of eyes, and sorrow of mind: And thy life shall hang in doubt before thee; and thou shalt fear day and night, and shalt have none assurance of thy life: In the morning thou shalt say, Would God it were even! and at even thou shalt say, Would God it were morning! for the fear of thine heart wherewith thou shalt fear, and for the sight of thine eyes which thou shalt see.

The Old Testament tells us how Israel broke the covenant and forfeited the divine blessing by their disobedience. The Davidic kingdom was divided into Northern and Southern Kingdoms after the death of Solomon. In 722-721 B.C. the Northern Kingdom was destroyed. In 586 B.C. the Southern Kingdom went into the Babylonian Captivity. A remnant of the Southern Kingdom returned to the land. Four hundred silent years ensued during which time there were no writing prophets, and God seemed far removed from the covenant people. Then Jesus, the incarnate Word, was born. He lived, died, and rose again. He ascended into heaven to await the time for the restitution of all things. But this Jesus who was rejected by Israel pronounced the words of divine judgment which are intimately connected with Deuteronomy 28.

Jesus told Israel that it would be dispersed among the nations. He promised that Jerusalem would be surrounded and the city taken. The city would fall into the hands of the Gentiles until the times of the Gentiles would come to an end (Luke 21:24). Josephus, the Jewish historian, has recorded for us what happened during the days of the siege in A.D. 70 when the armies of Rome plundered the city. The famine was so great that everything edible was consumed, including human flesh. The sack of the city was complete. Not one stone of Herod's Temple was left standing. The people were slain or carried away captive. The Gentiles took over Jerusalem and maintained their control of the city for almost two thousand years.

We must remember that this was the final prophetic dispersion of the Jews. In earlier times when the Northern and then the Southern Kingdom suffered under the assaults of Gentile powers, the people were distributed far and wide. At Pentecost when the Church was born, a million or more Jews from all over the Roman Empire assembled in Jerusalem for worship. But once Jerusalem was destroyed, there was no temple and no priesthood, no gathering of the Jews from around the Empire to celebrate their holy days. The Israelis were to be found as wanderers and outcasts all over the globe. The history of Judaism since then has been the story of the wandering Jews. They were persecuted wherever they went. They were brutalized, murdered, and stripped of their goods. They lived in ghettoes and were kept from intermingling with Gentiles in polite society. Even their livelihood was threatened. They were hated by the Church, which looked upon them as the murderers of Jesus, which they were. The whole burden of guilt for his death was falsely laid upon the Israelis as though all others in the world were guiltless. The fact is that the Romans were also implicated in that guilt. They crucified an innocent victim. And all of us were there when they crucified the Lord of Glory. We shouted with the multitudes, "Crucify him, crucify him." The guilt for the murder of Jesus was the guilt of all men, Israeli and Gentile alike.

God did stretch out his arm in punishment upon the people of his covenant. All that was spoken in Deuteronomy was, and is being, fulfilled to this very hour. The Israelis are still regarded as the pariahs of the earth. Anti-Semitism boils beneath the surface in every society. This has been going on for two thousand years and will continue until the end of the age. Then Israel at last will find deliverance when the regathered people of the Covenant turn to Jesus as their Messiah. We can ask the question why the Israelis have not turned to God in repentance and faith for two millennia. Paul wrote that "God hath given them the spirit of slumber, eyes that they should not see, and ears that they should not hear" (Rom. 11:8). Then he said "that blindness in part is happened to Israel, until the fulness of the Gentiles be come in" (Rom. 11:25). God in his sovereign grace has judicially blinded the eyes of his people Israel in the interest of the salvation of the Gentiles, of whom Paul says that the casting away of Israel is "the reconciling of the world" with Gentiles as a wild olive tree being grafted into the stock of Israel the true olive tree (Rom. 11:15-20).

During these two millennia the Israelis have maintained their separate identity in a peculiar fashion undreamed of and inexplicable from the human perspective. Not only has this been so, but the Israelis have continued to believe that Palestine belonged to them and that they would occupy it again in history. Through the centuries, the Israeli refrain has been, "Next year in Jerusalem." This city and this land have never been lost sight of by the Israelis. Here we must emphasize again that no one can understand the history of the world when sacred history or the unseen hand of God in history as revealed in Scripture is bypassed. God has put into the hearts of the Israelis this desire for Palestine. It cannot, and it will not, be eradicated. This is not to say that every Israeli shares this dream. But enough of them do, so that it will never die. The Orthodox Israelis, many of whom are looking for the coming of the Messiah, keep that vision, that dream of the promised land, in the foreview all the time. Even in boxcars as they were being shipped off to concentration camps their refrain as they sang the songs of Zion centered on the promise of God for their return to Jerusalem.

Toward the end of the nineteenth century, Zionism came into being in Europe. But long before this there was sporadic interest in a return to the land, and some Jews endeavored to create and support a Jewish national state in Palestine. Toward the end of the middle ages "messiahs" came forward to lead the Israelis back home. In the first part of the sixteenth century, David Reubeni and his disciple Solomon Molecho worked for a return to Palestine. In 1648, Sabbatai in Turkey proclaimed himself the Messiah. He later became a Muslim. During the first half of the nineteenth century, interest in the return of the Jews to Palestine was kept alive largely by Christian millennialists. Lord Shaftesbury and Sir Lawrence Oliphant sought to plant a Jewish state in Palestine but did not succeed. Mordecai Manuel Noah (1785-1851) a Jew from the United States publicized the idea of a Jewish return to Palestine.

Naftali Herz Imber (1856-1909), a Hebrew poet, was the author of *Hatikwa* ("The Hope"), a song which became a Zionist national anthem. He also wrote *Mishmar Hajardin* ("The Watch on the Jordan") which became a popular national-ist song. The novelist George Eliot encouraged a return to the land of Palestine in her book *Daniel Deronda* published in 1876. In 1862 Moses Hess (1812-1875) published a book which supplied the theoretical basis for Zionism. It was translated into English in 1918. In the book he combined ethical social-ism, fervent nationalism, and religious conservatism. He was a German Jew.

In the nineteenth century in Russia, the Jews were victims of a number of pogroms and otherwise suffered continuously from anti-Semitic persecutors. Numbers of Russians fled to the United States and small numbers went to Palestine. Toward the end of the century, an Austrian Jew from Vienna started what was to become the modern Zionist movement. His name was Theodor Herzl. He was to die at the early age of forty-four in 1904. He was a man with great charisma who sparked a revival of Jewish nationalism and was mourned perhaps more than any single Jew had been for centuries before that. Anti-Semitism was strong among the Germans of Austria so that Jews suffered. In August of 1897 Herzl put together the first Zionist congress, which convened in Basel, Switzerland. He also published *Die Welt* (*The World*) in the interest of Zionism.

In 1903 an event took place of historic importance. The father of Neville Chamberlain who went to Munich to meet with Hitler before World War II had the British government offer the Jews six thousand square miles of territory in Uganda where they could set up a Jewish state. A minority of the Zionists under Israel Zangwill were willing to accept the offer but the majority was against it. In effect the majority said: "We have waited two thousand years to go back to Palestine. Uganda is not Palestine. We will wait another two thousand years if we have to, to go back to the promised land." Such were the deeply held convictions of the Zionists. It must be remembered, however, that Zionism was more a political movement than a religious one. Today Zionism is a nationalistic movement, displaying little or no interest in the Old Testament Scriptures.

Another fortunate break in the move toward a return of the Jews to Palestine came in 1917. It was brought about through the efforts of Chaim Weizmann and Nahum Sokolow. Weizmann was a chemist who provided the British government with a formula for making nitroglycerin which was essential to the war effort, and particularly because of German U-Boat successes in the Atlantic which prevented the British from getting the supplies they needed from America. Lord (Arthur James) Balfour wrote a letter to Lord Rothschild, a Jew who was interested in and helped support Zionism or a return to Palestine, on November 2, 1917. The letter said:

> His Majesty's Government view with favour the establishment in Palestine of a national home for the Jewish people and will use their best endeavours to facilitate the achievement of this object, it being clearly understood that nothing shall be done which may prejudice the civil and religious rights of existing non-Jewish communities in Palestine or the rights and political status enjoyed by Jews in any other country.

In the settlement which followed World War I, the League of Nations which came into being made Palestine a British mandate. In 1914 the Jews had control of 177 square miles of Palestine. By 1935 under the British, the landed area was extended to 500 square miles. By 1935, 300,000 Jews were back in the land. It was World War II which marked the point of no return for the Jews in relation to Palestine. Anti-Semitism reached a peak under Adolph Hitler. Six million Jews were slaughtered in Hitler's death camps. The number is disputed by some, but of this there can be no doubt: millions of Jews did die. In Poland, for example, there were several million Jews. Of that number only 15,000 are known to be in Poland today. Auschwitz and Treblinka, among others, remain to haunt the memories of the nations for what was done in those murder camps. Taken intact before the war ended, they are museums of murder which millions of people have traversed since then. Germany was also emptied of its Jewish population by Hitler and his executioners. The massacre of so many Jews aided the cause of a Jewish return to Palestine as a homeland.

The United Nations came into being after World War II. On May 14, 1948 the State of Israel with its six-pointed star was born. The United States recognized the new state immediately. Other nations followed, but there still are many nations which have refused to recognize Israel's existence and sovereignty. War after war was fought by the Arabs to eject the Jews from Israel. The Israeli state grew larger, rather than smaller, as the Jewish people were victors again and again. The United States, then and now, has been Israel's best friend. Billions of dollars of American money have been poured into Israel. The United States has supplied that nation with armaments with which to defend its borders.

In the recent war with Egypt the Israelis emerged triumphant. They also seized a vast acreage of additional territory. Under more recent arrangements with the Egyptian government, much of the confiscated land has been returned to Egyptian sovereignty. The war in Palestine produced a somewhat strange result. Hundreds of thousands of Arabs who had occupied Palestine for centuries became refugees. Whereas the Jews had been refugees seeking a homeland, the acquisition of a homeland produced Arab refugees. The surrounding Arab countries did nothing to provide a homeland for the refugees. One result was the emergence of the Palestinian Liberation Organization (The PLO) which has for its goal the reacquisition of the lands the Arabs lost to the Israelis. The PLO has stated again and again that it intends to drive the Israelis into the sea. In other words, they have said they will exterminate the Israelis when and if they can. Whether this is only rhetoric and can be resolved peacefully remains to be seen.

Recent changes in the Near East, such as the overthrow of the Shah in Iran and the Russian occupation of Afghanistan, have made the situation more difficult. It appears that the United States will pressure the Israeli government to make a deal with the PLO, returning some land on the west bank to the displaced peoples. If a new Arab state should be set up there, it will imbalance the military situation and leave an Arab dagger pointed at the heart of the Israeli state if the PLO should decide for war rather than peace. Israel has been placed in a very exposed position for several reasons. It has little or no oil of its own at this point, and is thus dependent on oil from the United States. The Arab oil powers are not friendly toward Israel and probably will not supply that nation with oil. Israel also suffers from raging inflation. In the year 1979 it was at 110%. In February 1980 the state issued a new currency. Inflation presents a grave threat to the financial integrity of the country. Moreover, it is surrounded by Arab nations who outnumber the Israelis by forty to one. In addition to this, Israel is faced with the hatred of the Soviet Union and its captive nations. This is important from the perspective of biblical prophecy as we shall see in a moment.

The return of the Jews to the land was significant. But from the standpoint of biblical prophecy the capture of Jerusalem was more significant. When the Israelis secured control of the old city of Jerusalem, Gentile dominion over the city ended after two thousand years. This was both a blessing and a problem. It so happens that Jerusalem is a sacred city to Christians, and to the Arabs as well as to the Jews. The mosque on the Dome of the Rock is second only to Mecca in the minds of the Muslims. It was here that Abraham was supposed to have offered up Isaac as a sacrifice. Abraham is the father of the Arab peoples through Ishmael even as he is father of the Israelis through Isaac and Jacob.

The Rabbinate of Jerusalem forbids Jews to traverse the land on which this Muslim mosque rests. It is also sacred to the Jews because it was thought to be the site on which the Solomonic Temple was built. Efforts to internationalize the city of Jerusalem have not succeeded. The Muslims want to wrest the control of the city from the hands of the Jews. The Jews stubbornly refuse to let go. The problem appears to be impossible to resolve.

It is no accident that the cauldron is boiling in the Near East. Nor is it any accident that so many competing forces seek to control the city of Jerusalem and the land of Palestine itself. Nor can we forget that everybody involved believes that the side he represents is in the right and has a legitimate claim to the land. It is hard to imagine that anyone's claim will be surrendered. On January 16, 1980 Prime Minister Menachem Begin rendered a report to the Israeli Knesset about his talks with President Sadat at Aswan. He was explicit when the subject of Jerusalem was broached. He said:

> Regarding Jerusalem, I did not hold back my reply for even an instant. No practical proposal was put forward, but Jerusalem was mentioned in the talks. And I immediately told President Sadat that our stand is known to him—and he noted that he knows it—and I also read to him my letter to the President of the United States. *The capital of Israel is not divisible.* Free access to members of all religions to their holy places, as anchored in the law—thus it will be forever. That is our stand and thus it will remain.

This much is clear. Israel will not surrender one inch of land in Jerusalem. It will remain under Israeli control now and forever. This does not exclude, of course, the forceful takeover of the city by armed force. But it will only come about by conquest after the last Israeli guarding the sacred city has been killed.

Prime Minister Begin also spoke about the invasion of Afghanistan by the Soviet Union. He mentioned the "Breshnev Doctrine" by which, should any danger be posed to what is termed a socialist regime within the sphere of Soviet control, the Soviet Union has the right to employ military measures." He spoke of the shameful assertion that Soviet interference in Afghanistan was an "assistance to a friend." Then he observed:

> If a Soviet invasion is assistance to a friend what, God forbid, would be liable to happen were a so-called Palestinian state to be established in Eretz Israel, or a similar creation under the rule of the Kaddoumis and the Arafats. Within a very short time it would become a Soviet base— at the invitation of a friend. The flight time from Odessa to Eretz Israel is just a few hours. And certainly what has taken place close to our region is liable to take place in our region, in the heart of the Middle East. For us this would pose a threat to our very existence. . . . So let all nations beware—where this region is concerned also—and

understand why we unreservedly reject not only the establishment of a Palestinian state, but also the formation of a corridor liable to lead to it. For this is the common danger faced by all the free people.

Prime Minister Begin made mention of

Jordan's equipping itself with advanced weaponry, the presence of Russians and Cubans in South Yemen, the strange and shocking incident in Mecca, involving the desecration of Islam's holiest place, which according to the practitioners of the big lie in our time was perpetrated by Americans and Israelis, the sale of sophisticated American arms to Saudi Arabia, Libya's becoming a huge Soviet arsenal and more. . . .

There can be no doubt that Israel is keenly aware of the fragile position it occupies in the Middle East. It is entrenched there, but for how long? With collusion between the PLO and the Soviets, and with what has happened in Afghanistan and might happen in Iran, the Israelis are alert to the dangers they face. In two thousand years of history since the crucifixion and resurrection of Jesus, there has been no situation comparable to what we see today. For those of us who look upon secular history from the divine standpoint what does all of this mean?

With Israel back in the land and in control of Jerusalem, it is virtually impossible to think that this is anything other than the fulfillment of biblical prophecy. Gentile ascendancy has ended over Jerusalem. This is one of the signs of the times indicating that the return of the Lord is near. The existence of the State of Israel is also a sign of the times. The Book of Zechariah makes plain that Israel and Jerusalem will be sieged at the end of the age. In chapter 14, the Scripture says:

Behold, the day of the Lord cometh, and thy spoil shall be divided in the midst of thee. For I will gather all nations against Jerusalem to battle; and the city shall be taken, and houses rifled, and the women ravished; and half of the city shall go forth into captivity, and the residue of the people shall not be cut off from the city. Then shall the Lord go forth, and fight against those nations, as when he fought in the day of battle. And his feet shall stand in that day upon the mount of Olives, which is before Jerusalem

> on the east, and the mount of Olives shall cleave in the midst thereof toward the east and toward the west [14:1-4].

None of the events predicted in Zechariah has taken place at an earlier time. These events are associated with the coming of the Lord. We are told that "in that day shall the Lord defend the inhabitants of Jerusalem; and he that is feeble among them at that day shall be as David; and the house of David shall be as God, as the angel of the Lord before them" (12:8).

The Scriptures which foretell the return of the Jews to Israel have enjoyed a remarkable fulfillment. There are many Jews, however, who have not returned to Palestine. Scripture does not tell us what proportion of the Jews must come back before the end of history takes place. It does say that they shall be gathered from the east and the west, the north and the south. There are now more Jews in the United States than in Israel. Does this mean that large numbers of Jews must emigrate from the United States to Israel? I do not know. Nor does the Word of God make this plain. It appears unreasonable to think that the State of Israel would be able to care for the influx if the Jews of America left this nation en masse.

The Jews who have formed the State of Israel have returned to the land in unbelief. Thus we can say that the return has not been based upon explicit obedience to the Word of God, nor does it mean that many of the Jews in Israel are devout or religious. Zionism is political, and so many of the Jews are purely secular. The State of Israel is not friendly toward what is called proselytism, and restrictions against the propagation of the Christian faith and against genuine religious freedom have increased. Yet the best friends of Israel have been evangelicals who are looking for the coming of the Lord and who believe that Israel will play a vital role in the end times.

Pro-Israel sentiment among evangelicals has inclined them to exhibit a certain amount of animosity toward the Arabs. They have supported the Israeli claims to the land of Palestine and in so doing have opened themselves to criticism by those who favor the Arabs and who feel that a great injustice has been done to them. It must not be forgotten that God is also concerned for the Arabs, and the Scripture foretells a time when the enemies of Israel will be at peace with her. Isaiah says:

In that day there shall be a highway out of Egypt to
Assyria, and the Assyrian shall come into Egypt, and the
Egyptian into Assyria, and the Egyptians shall serve with
the Assyrians.

In that day Israel shall be the third with Egypt and with
Assyria, even a blessing in the midst of the land: whom
the Lord of hosts shall bless, saying, Blessed be Egypt
my people, and Assyria the work of my hands, and Israel
mine inheritance [Isa. 19:23-25].

There is no reason to believe that anyone will get the Jews
out of Palestine. This must mean that the fig tree is beginning
to bud. Those things which are happening allow us to conclude that the Lord will come before this generation passes
from the scene.

We live in exciting times, albeit difficult ones, but the soon
coming of Jesus is enough to take all fear from us and leave us
with great assurance that the peace men have dreamed about
for ages will soon be upon us. But it will be a peace which
comes from God, not from sinful men, not from the Church,
not from the Jews, but from the Lord God Almighty. And the
return of the Jews to Palestine and the end of Gentile rule over
Jerusalem constitute the most positive evidences that we are,
or will be shortly, in the closing days of this age.

3

WORLD CONDITIONS A SIGN OF CHRIST'S COMING

THE PRESIDENT OF THE UNITED STATES, ONCE A YEAR in January, reports to the Congress on the state of the union. Any thoughtful review of the state of the nation and the state of affairs around the world must lead to the conclusion that never before in man's history has the situation been so grave, so threatening, and so filled with evil portents. The hearts of men everywhere are filled with fear.

Surely world conditions have been bad in times past, but never has there been a situation such as we have today. In other ages segments of the world suffered from wars, dislocation, natural disasters, and economic slumps. But other areas of the planet then were unaffected by what was happening in places far removed from them. Four explosions which have taken place in the last hundred years account for what now exists among the nations of the world.

The population of the world has increased so significantly that catastrophe may occur in the near future. By A.D. 2000 the population of the world will increase by a third—by two billion more people, at a time when resources are shrinking, food supplies, and the distribution of those supplies are inadequate, and the poorer nations are getting poorer each day.

The second explosion is the transportation explosion. For nineteen hundred years the means of transportation remained the same. People traveled on foot, by donkey and horseback, by carriage, and by small boats. Today we can travel by planes with speeds exceeding two thousand miles an hour and by spaceships which travel twenty thousand miles an hour. On the planning boards are vehicles intended to travel one hundred thousand miles an hour. Interplanetary travel and trips to the moon are already facts.

The third explosion relates to communications. We know what is taking place anywhere in the world almost immediately via radio, television, telephone, and telegraph. The world has become so small that the vibrations of revolution in the smallest nation are felt instantly around the world and have an impact on all of us. The United Nations has in its membership nations smaller than New Jersey in size and with populations fewer in number than some of America's smaller states. They speak and act in the United Nations with a clout far exceeding their intrinsic strength. And a combination of tiny sovereign states can and do shake the largest nations of the organization.

The fourth explosion involves the accretion of human knowledge. In the past quarter of a century, the world has more than doubled all the knowledge it had gathered in all the earlier ages of history. The amount of knowledge will be doubled or tripled again before the end of this century. Computer technology, which is still in its infancy, has become ingrained in all of man's activities and makes possible the storage and retrieval of information on a scale undreamed of thirty years ago. This technological advance is fraught with great possibilities for good as well as great potential for untold evil.

We only need to mention a few of the technocratic breakthroughs to demonstrate how great has been the progress among nations in the last hundred years. Electricity, railroads, automobiles, radio, telegraph, television, nuclear weaponry, telephones, high speed presses, computer technology, airplanes, spaceships, laser beams, microfilm, and a thousand other inventions have altered the patterns of life for everyone around the world. All of this makes it possible for us to understand better what at one time was a seemingly impossible prophetic word about the coming of the Lord: "Every eye shall see him, and they also which pierced him" (Rev. 1:7).

A quick look at the political, economic, social, and religious conditions around the globe shows convincingly how close the coming of the Lord may be. For the world situation approximates more closely than ever before what Scripture describes the characteristics of the end of the age will be like.

POLITICAL CONDITIONS

Jesus said, "Ye shall hear of wars and rumours of wars ... for all these things must come to pass, but the end is not yet. For nation shall rise against nation, and kingdom against kingdom" (Matt. 24:6, 7). Never has the political situation described more closely approximated what is happening among the nations today.

Politically, the nations of the world for centuries have operated on the basis of what is called the balance of power. By this we mean that nations whose aspirations were in conflict with other nations would bring into being coalitions designed to create a balance of power by both sides to keep the stronger military alliance from decimating the weaker one. A maxim of geopolitics is that whenever one side becomes significantly weaker than its enemy, the stronger side will seek to annihilate the weaker one. The balance of power game was used in the Old Testament again and again. For example, in 2 Chronicles 20, the Scriptures speak of a coalition of powers formed against Judah. Included in the coalition were Moab, Ammon, "and with them other beside the Ammonites" (2 Chron. 20:1). God defeated the military coalition and Judah survived. In the days of Nebuchadnezzar, Judah wanted to seek by treaty the aid of Egypt to offset the power of Babylon. Again and again in the history of the divided kingdom, Israel and Judah sought alliances of a military nature to protect themselves.

Today the world has been divided into two major opposing coalitions. The western democracies have the North Atlantic Treaty Organization and the Soviet Union has the Warsaw Pact. Unaligned nations, while not partners in these pacts, have indicated their preferences for one or the other of the two parties. India, for example, seems to have cast its lot within the Warsaw orbit. The People's Republic of China is seeking rapprochement with the United States against the Soviet Union. All over the globe, communism seeks to extend its power, and will do so unless the offsetting power of NATO can effectively prevent it. No greater imperialism can be found than that which characterizes the Soviet Union. She has extended her sovereignty over many nations such as Poland, Finland, East Germany, Czechoslovakia, Hungary, Cuba, and more recently has invaded and is devastating Afghanistan. The Bear is moving forward steadily, absorbing more and more territory around the globe. The western democracies are fighting a rearguard action and are losing ground almost everywhere.

Through Cuba, the Soviet Union has effectively destabilized Central and Latin America. Right now most of Central America is under the thumb of communism or shortly will be.

Latin American countries for the most part are dictatorships, and governments are being overthrown all the time. In the Middle East, the Soviets have moved aggressively into the Arab world for several reasons. During this present decade, the Soviet Union will need oil supplies far beyond its current capacity to produce that energy in its own empire. Russia will move into the Arab oil areas to take by force what it cannot obtain by peaceful means. The recent occupation of Afghanistan poses a serious threat to Iran, which is unstable and hardly able to defend itself. Russia has penetrated into the Gulf of Aden and the gulf of Oman, and has sent a fleet of naval vessels into the Indian Ocean and Arabian Sea. If it succeeds in its objectives, it will be able to control the flow of oil by tankers to western Europe, the United States, and Japan. If middle eastern oil were to be cut off from the industrial nations, the resultant shortage would be catastrophic.

Russia has long coveted a warm water port in the south, both in the Black Sea and now in the area of the Arabian Sea. Turkey is in gross disarray, and although a member of NATO, it appears open to subversion by the Soviets. If the Black Sea is ever opened to the Soviets, it will curb the usefulness of the Suez Canal. And if the Arabian gulf (the Persian Gulf) falls under Soviet control, it will effectively block off all the oil exports from this region at the will of Russia. It is almost impossible to overstress the significance of these movements by the Soviets in the Middle East.

Vietnam and Cambodia, where millions of people have been slaughtered by the communists, and Thailand are pivotal areas in southeast Asia which are under the guns of the communists. South Korea faces a hostile communist North Korea with the expectation that war could break out at any time between a free south and a communist north.

In Africa, revolutions have been endemic for several decades. Nation after nation has gained independence, and numbers of them are now under communist control. To the north of South Africa, a belt of nations going from the east to the west cut off South Africa, which is under attack because of its racism and because it is a bastion of white domination in a continent that is dominantly black. Rhodesia has come under the sway of communists. In the struggle for transition from white to black control of the nation, the dominant largest parties in control of the country are leftists who enjoy the support and backing of the communist world. Ethiopia was destabilized and has been rendered ineffective with the almost certain expectation that the communists will control that nation.

Vis-a-vis the United States, the Soviet Union has acquired a military superiority which suggests that the balance of power has shifted in favor of the Soviets and may lead inexorably to military adventurism by them, which could bring on World War III. Alexander Solzhenitsyn has argued forcefully that World War III is already in progress on a smaller scale and that the West is losing that war day by day. The Soviet Union is noted for signing treaties, none of which it keeps. Salt I has been broken again and again by them. Salt II, if it is ever approved by the Senate of the United States, will be broken before the ink is dry on the paper. The West seems incapable of thinking in terms other than those which reflect their own understanding of ethics. The Soviets look at ethics from a totally different perspective and unless the West understands how the Soviet mind works, it will be the loser every time.

China represents an unknown factor in the world of politics. But let it never be forgotten that Red China is committed to Marxism-Leninism. This commitment means that its foundational principles are antithetical to those on which western democracy is based. It is a good Marxist principle to be friends with your enemy when you need his help against another enemy. But when the other enemy is overcome, you revert to your old relationship with the "friend" who has helped you and whom you will now seek to overthrow as well. Red China has not yet acquired parity with the major powers because it is still a backward nation. But it is an energetic nation with a wealth of manpower exceeded by no other nation in the world. It has been estimated that fifty million Chinese were slaughtered by the communists after they had gained control of the nation. China could afford to lose two hundred million people in war if necessary and would still emerge as a superpower in human resources. Give or take a few decades and Red China will become one of the most influential nations in world politics. And it is just as anti-God, anti-West, antidemocractic, and anticapitalistic as the Soviet Union.

Red China and the Soviet Union represent competitive communist systems. The Soviets support Vietnam and have helped that nation subdue Laos and now Cambodia. At the time of this writing, it is possible that Vietnam may invade Thailand and thus control the Straits of Malacca, establishing a new Indo-Chinese empire such as that of the French before it was forced to evacuate the region. If this occurs, the empire will be subject to Soviet influence and will earn the enmity of Red China, which already has taken military action against Vietnam ostensibly to "teach them a lesson" or more important perhaps to test their own weaponry and troops in actual combat.

In Britain, the battle continues to rage against the IRA, which has for its objective the takeover of Northern Ireland, which is dominantly Protestant. It would be joined to Ireland to form a consolidated nation state. The attempt has been based on terrorism leading to the murder of many people. The IRA has the support of many Irishmen in the United States, especially in the Boston area. But the IRA is left wing and has received covert help from the Soviets, who seek to destabilize Great Britain. The terrorism in Northern Ireland is an old form of warfare on a more sophisticated level than heretofore. It has been used in Germany, Italy, and Latin America in a variety of forms. Terrorism has been extended to a level where it has become an international *cause celebre*. The seizure of the United States embassy in Tehran and the capture of fifty Americans who have been held hostage for a long period of time is an indicator of how serious this form of terrorism has become. Other embassies and other diplomatic personnel have been seized and murdered around the world. There no longer seems to be any respect for international law. In the case of Iran, the action was condemned by the United Nations, but Iran has not been expelled from the UN nor have the efforts of this organization been successful in securing the release of the captives at the time of this writing.

In Italy, the terrorists who have attacked businessmen as well as political leaders have shattered the kneecaps of their victims, crippling them for life, or have shot them dead. In some cases, ransoms have been paid which only gives the terrorists funding for further depredations. Airplane hijacking has been used extensively so that the cost of checking passengers in terminals before they board planes has added considerably to the cost of plane fares. There is no reason to suppose that terrorism in its manifold forms will cease. Rather it can be expected to increase in numbers, severity, and variety in the years ahead. Given the availability of weaponry, terrorism will prove to be a thorn in the side of every legitimate government.

The constant and increasing threat of the use of nuclear weaponry continues to alarm and harass the nations. As more and more nations succeed in detonating atom bombs, the greatest likelihood of their use lies in sudden and unexpected attacks or in nuclear blackmail. The first strike potential of nuclear weapons could result in the death of hundreds of millions of people. The threat boggles the mind and raises the question whether man could resort to the use of this awful instrument of destruction. But when Hitler and Stalin come to memory, and their callous resort to the murder of millions of people is taken into account, no one can suppose that there will not be some madman in the future who would not hesitate to push the nuclear button. Also, it is almost impossible not to believe that the Israelis, given their great gifts, possess atom and hydrogen bombs. They have not, and will not, forget the Holocaust. Nor is there the slightest possibility that they will forego the use of these weapons *if* they again face genocide. "Never again, another Auschwitz" is and will be an Israeli slogan for as long as time exists.

Nuclear weaponry is not all that men have to fear. Germ warfare and the use of noxious chemicals cannot be discounted. If they were used in water supplies, multitudes could die in a short time. When the Soviet troops entered Afghanistan they did not hesitate to use Napalm to exterminate some of the citizens of that country, and in March of 1980, reports filtered through of their intention to stay there for a long time. And nobody stands ready to oppose this war of conquest. Cosmic rays and laser beams promise to add other instruments of death to the arsenals of the nations. Every day additional knowledge is gained which will intensify the possibilities for creating even more terrible agents of death and destruction. Is it any wonder, then, that we conclude that world political conditions constitute a visible signal of the impending coming of the Lord Jesus Christ?

ECONOMIC CONDITIONS

Once men enter into fraternal relations with other men, economics becomes important because they also enter into relations with others in the exchange of commodities, property, and the sale of goods and services wherever and whenever these things are desirable. In order for these economic relationships to prosper, there must exist some medium of exchange which can be used to buy and sell goods and services. From time immemorial, gold and silver have been the media most widely accepted and used. It is true that nothing in itself has value except as men impart value to this or that particular medium for exchange purposes. Once men begin buying and selling from each other, they discover that to exchange salt for wheat or potatoes for a dress is severely limited unless and until they have a medium of exchange. This medium, call it money, which has value in it to the person who receives it is used in exchange for goods or services. The seller then can use that medium of exchange to buy something he wants but which he could not get from the man who bought his potatoes or salt.

Silver and gold became the media of exchange for several reasons. First, they were scarce. Who would regard pebbles and grains of sand as media of exchange? Secondly, these metals were imperishable. Thirdly, most men everywhere were ready and willing to use them. When paper money came into being, it usually represented gold and silver hidden in some safe place. But the paper money could be exchanged for gold or silver upon demand of the possessor of the paper money. Paper money, however, never had any intrinsic value in itself. It was good so long as the possessor knew he could redeem the paper with the two metals. But once the amount of paper money exceeded the supply of silver and gold, it meant that paper money became less valuable. The more paper money there was in circulation vis-a-vis the supply of gold and silver, the more paper money was demanded for an ounce of silver or gold. This is what inflation is all about.

Inflation is one of the leading economic problems faced by the world today. Because trade is international, currencies of each nation must be exchanged with differing values attached to each currency. Today the economic situation has become grave due to balance of payment deficits of nations like the United States. A balance of payments deficit occurs when a nation buys from others more than they sell to them and gives them paper money in exchange. As long as a nation can exchange whatever paper money they hold for gold or silver, it has confidence in any nation's paper money. But when it can no longer do this, sooner or later the price must be paid for that failure: either the nation's paper money becomes less valuable and sellers will increase the prices of the goods they sell to that nation or they refuse to sell their goods for less valuable paper money. Inflation is rampant around the world today. The American dollar, faced by double digit inflation, and probably by triple digit inflation in a short time, has lost ninety-five percent of its purchasing power across the years.

The national debt of the United States continues to rise and by 1981 will be ranging closer and closer to one trillion dollars. In 1979, the interest payments on the national debt amounted to over fifty-six billions of dollars. The National Taxpayers' Union has computed the financial obligations of the United States to be more than nine trillions of dollars, or about $113,000 per taxpayer. In March of 1980, interest rates had risen to twenty percent and housing loans to fifteen and one-half percent. Social services were the largest single item in the federal budget, exceeding military spending and all other items. The nation was well on its way to bankruptcy and this fact posed the possibility of a takeover by the Soviet Union, whose military supremacy vis-a-vis the NATO nations is common knowledge and seen as a grave danger by the generals and admirals of the U. S. armed forces.

Last year the inflation rate for Israel was 110 percent. Early in 1980 it printed a new currency and called in the old on a ten to one basis. In some Latin American countries the inflation rate runs two or three or four hundred percent a year. There is a grave international money crisis which is going to get worse. And everybody will suffer. Americans today are angry with the oil producing nations (OPEC) because they have raised their prices for oil so much in recent years. The anger should be directed at the American government which has been printing too much paper money. The Arab nations, among other reasons, seem to have wisely tied the price of their oil to the number of American dollars needed to buy an ounce of gold or silver. Oil, priced relative to these metals, costs no more than it did fifteen or twenty years ago. The misdirected anger toward the oil-producing nations could possibly lead to military confrontation. This might be of great importance to the people of the State of Israel. It can be explained easily. Suppose for a moment that Japan with its hundred or so millions of people were to be faced with a choice between getting no oil from the Arab nations or leaving Israel at the mercy of the Arabs in return for which they would get the oil they needed. Israel with its several million Jews would be weighed over against the economic plight of more than a hundred million Japanese. There is no doubt what the Japanese would do if they were faced with economic chaos occasioned by the lack of oil. Once they knew they could get oil if they agreed to let the Arabs do as they pleased with regard to Israel, they would choose oil, not Israel.

The United States has generously helped the Israelis with money, oil, and armaments. But if the economic survival of almost two hundred and fifty million Americans was at stake because of the refusal of the Arab oil nations to keep it supplied with the amount of oil it needs for its industry, there is a real possibility that America would choose Arab oil and leave Israel in the lurch. In the plainest language possible, we must say that the economic situation is dynamically related to political matters and the closing days of the present age will make this very clear.

The Bible states that in the last days men will not be able to buy or sell unless they bear the mark of the beast. This describes the coming crisis when the beast will exercise economic control over the destinies of the nations. It is an unpleasant thought. But more than that, it tells us something about the loss of three basic freedoms intrinsic to democratic capitalism over against oppressive and unjust socialism: (1) freedom or the right to life, as well as freedom of movement including the right to leave one nation for another; (2) the right to engage in economic trade and relations with other people; and (3) the imprescriptible right to the ownership of private property. These are man's essential freedoms. They are not freedoms given to man by legislative fiat or conveyed to man by other men. They are basic rights which exist in the creation ordinances of God for man. Man has them because God has given them to him. These rights have been eroded and indeed taken from men wherever communism has assumed control. No man in the Soviet Union can own a farm. And if he did, he would be prevented from selling his produce to other people. No Soviet citizen can live in Moscow without a permit from the government. And the government can ship him off to Siberia or take his life for any pretext. Everyone is a slave under communism except those who have obtained the power which they use to deprive all other men of their three basic freedoms.

No one who lives in a democracy should suppose for one moment that his freedoms exist so that he can exercise his rights without fear of reprisal. Wage and price controls, for example, deprive man of economic freedom. Rationing is another device which takes freedom from the governed. The right to life has already been taken away from fetal life in the womb. Millions of unborn infants are aborted around the world every year and the right to life denied them. This is a right taken from the unborn that those who are alive still try to preserve for infants no longer in their mothers' wombs. Why is it right to protect a two-day-old baby from being murdered, but wrong to prevent a fetus of three or four months from being wiped out through abortion?

When the American government can set the price for oil taken from American wells, it is taking money from the pockets of the owners of those wells. When it raises the price of domestically-produced oil, and then exacts an excess profits tax, which simply does the same thing in a slightly different way, is this just? It destroys the imprescriptible right to private property and saps the foundation of democratic capitalism which has done more for mankind than any system, any time, anywhere around the globe. This is simply another indicator of the end times, and of the ever-tightening noose being thrown around the necks of men whose freedoms are being eroded and who will shortly come under the sovereignty of the Antichrist in the last days.

Gustave LeBon was the author of *The Psychology of Socialism* and *The Psychology of Revolutions*. He hated tyranny in all of its forms, recognized the dilemmas faced by democratic societies, yet understood that:

> in spite of all the difficulties attending their functioning, parliamentary assemblies are the best form of government mankind has discovered as yet, and more especially the best means it has found to escape the yoke of personal tyrannies. Moreover, in reality, they present only two serious dangers, one being inevitable financial waste, and the other the progressive restriction of the liberty of the individual.

He noted that:

> Socialism whose dream is to substitute itself for the ancient faiths, proposes only a very low ideal, and to establish it appeals to sentiments lower still. . . . With what lever does it seek to raise the soul? With the sentiments of envy and hatred it creates in the hearts of the multitudes. To the crowd, no longer satisfied with the political and civic equality, it proposes equality of condition, without dreaming that social inequalities are born of those natural inequalities that man has always been powerless to change.

And he concluded that:

> Democracy, by its very principles, favors the liberty and competition which of necessity lead to the triumph of the most capable, while socialism, on the contrary, aims at the suppression of competition, the disappearance of liberty, and a general equalization, so that there is evidently an insuperable opposition between the principles of socialism and those of democracy.

If democratic capitalism were unleashed, the world would be fed and the material conditions of men improved everywhere. It will not happen, given the temper of the times, and this movement to socialism so prominent in western society. The situation as it is in communist nations gives us every reason to believe that the dictatorship promised in Scripture in the end times may not be very far off.

SOCIAL CONDITIONS

Social conditions are interwoven with economic and political conditions. They cannot be considered in isolation from these other factors. Thus the reader must bear in mind the interrelationships even if it seems that we are talking exclusively about social concerns.

The family as the basic unit of society is in the process of being destroyed for many. This is particularly true for the western world. In an affluent society in which secularism places a high premium on possessions, husbands and wives must find their means of livelihood in the marketplace. The mother leaves the house at eight in the morning and returns at five or six o'clock in the evening. The children are on their own without parental guidance for the better part of the day. Father and mother must then take care of household matters without many hours left for raising their children. The television set has become the baby-sitter. Studies already show that more hours are spent looking at television than in any other pursuit. The omnipresence of TV with sports, specials, news, soap operas, crime, and mind-conditioning programs staggers the imagination.

Divorce is a second potent factor in the breakdown of the family. Forty percent of all marriages in America will end in divorce. The percentage may increase gradually. Many families have his children, her children and their children. In addition, hundreds of thousands of men and women live together without the benefit of matrimony, ready to break off a temporary alliance according to whim or wish. Millions of children are being raised in an environment which encourages the idea of divorce for any reason and which virtually guarantees that future generations of young people will pursue the same pattern.

Fornication, adultery, homosexuality and perverse sexual exploits not to be mentioned in polite society abound everywhere. What is more troublesome is the claim that these sins against nature and God constitute legitimate and legal options as well as spiritually-approved alternatives. The sense of sin has disappeared among large segments of society in these days. Paul described these conditions aptly two thousand years ago when he wrote:

... men shall be lovers of their own selves, covetous, boasters, proud, blasphemers, disobedient to parents, unthankful, unholy, without natural affection, trucebreakers, false accusers, incontinent, fierce, despisers of those that are good, traitors, heady, highminded, lovers of pleasure more than lovers of God; having a form of godliness, but denying the power thereof: from such turn away. For of this sort are they which creep into houses, and lead captive silly women laden with sins, led away with divers lusts, ever learning, and never able to come to the knowledge of the truth [2 Tim. 3:1-7].

A black commentator, William Raspberry, in a column printed in the *Los Angeles Times*, (Jan. 25, 1980, Part II, p. 9) agreed with Professor Edward A. Wynne that America has produced a "generation of self-centered, withdrawn, unsympathetic, irreligious, unpatriotic and characterless young people." The professor also said "The statistics reveal steady increases in adolescent conduct which can be described as either other-destructive or self-destructive." The accompanying statistics are frightening:

Deaths by homicide of white males aged 15 to 19 increased from 2.7 per 100,000 in 1959 to 7.5 per 100,000 in 1976—an increase of 177 percent (The previous high in the century was 5.2 in 1919.)

Between 1950 and 1976, the annual suicide rate for young white males rose from 3.5 per 100,000 to 11.9—an increase of 260 percent.

In addition, there is statistical evidence of major increases in the youthful abuse of illicit drugs and alcohol, in sexual promiscuity, in illegitimacy, and in venereal disease.

The same *Los Angeles Times* printed a Reuters report (Feb. 2, 1980, Part I, p. 3) that "Britons drank more than 92 million gallons of wine in 1978, twice as much as in 1968. Liquor consumption has also doubled since 1968. The report said divorces in England and Wales in 1977 were almost three times the rate of 1968."

These gloomy statistics do not pertain only to nations of the west. The communist countries are also experiencing similar trends. Juvenile crime, hooliganism, alcoholism, and crime abound in the Soviet Union. Drug addiction is common everywhere and it always brings with it high crime rates, a result of the need for money to support the drug habit. What may be even worse than these alarming statistics is the rise of the welfare state, which has created masses of dependent people who stay on welfare for life. They have been emptied of their self-respect, and reproduce their own kind as one generation of children after another stays on public welfare from the womb to the tomb. They compose a growing proportion of the population in the United States at least to a point where the end of public welfare would probably create a revolutionary situation. This social monstrosity has political ramifications, for the parasites who feed on the public purse (which consumes the fruit of the labor of those who are gainfully employed) vote for whoever will increase their benefits and most surely would vote against those who intended to end those benefits.

C. S. Lewis in his little book, *The Abolition of Man,* spelled out for all to see this emasculation of which I speak. Men cease to be men. Instead, they become faceless, thoughtless, nameless victims of do-gooders who empty them of self-respect, dull the sense of the image of God in them, and make them at last no better than animals running to the feed pens when the cymbals clang and the whistles blow. With the destruction of their selfhood, such people are ready for exploitation by the Antichrist, whose mark they will gladly bear so long as he feeds, clothes, warms, and gives them television, circuses, and sports events to keep them occupied. What the welfare state does is different from what the Soviet Union does to men, but in the end the result is the same for either. Men cease to be men, losing those human characteristics and forsaking any decent world and life view that once distinguished men from pigs and horses.

The dump heap of history is filled with the corpses of men and nations who have gone this route before. The difference in the world situation today from those in bygone days is the magnitude of the problem, that is the scale it has reached, which far exceeds anything the world has ever known. Another difference is the universal nature of the tragedy.

Whereas in former ages the downfall of nations transpired within a limited geographical area, today it covers the planet and is growing in intensity.

This examination of the social conditions of the age can be summarized by remarks made by Alvin Toffler, the futurist whose book *Future Shock* shook the world a few years ago. What he said interpenetrates the economic and political spheres which, in turn, help to shape the social situation of the world. Toffler said there had been two earlier waves of what he called "progress." The first was when "people abandoned caves to live in communal societies." The second was the Industrial Revolution. Now he sees the advent of the third wave in which

> the current crises plaguing the world's energy supplies, money markets, education and family, indicate an eventual breakdown of the traditional industrial system, and the "leap to a new stage of technological evolution."
>
> Ninety-nine percent of all science and technology is that which has been developed for the rich, and that's a frightening realization. Unless we make the computer into a cheap, simple, and easy-to-use tool for the entire world, we risk losing it.

Unfortunately, Toffler is committed to an evolutionary view of life and looks for a quantum leap to a still higher stage of human development. He does not allow for a sovereign God at work on the world's problems, nor does he reveal any apparent knowledge of the breakthrough which is coming shortly and will indeed be cataclysmic, violent, and cosmic in nature. For the very marks that he perceives to exist in the structure of things today are the signs to which Christians point as evidence that we may be in the closing days of the present age and the soon coming of Jesus Christ.

RELIGIOUS CONDITIONS

Despite the claims to the contrary, man's religious condition is not the result of his economic, political, and social views. Such a statement, on the surface, is nonsense to most people today. Why? Because the world in which we live has largely been secularized. And the secularization of the world has resulted in the secularization of many Christians as well. Unfortunately, few Christians think Christianly even though they are genuine Christians so far as the new birth is concerned. But they do not think as Christians ought to think. The secularization process has reached the point where religion is looked upon by many as an outdated anachronism, an invention of little minds who do not have the courage to be heroic without some god to worship. The secular mind has little use for the man who must be dependent on something or someone outside of himself. This is the tragedy of our age. Man thinks he can go it alone.

The secular mind is all too often the atheist mind. Until recently, virtually all men worshiped some god. Atheism represented a small minority of the world's people. The onward march of atheism is another indicator of the soon coming of Christ. The Soviet Union and Red China together represent two large nations officially bound by atheist convictions. When the smaller communist nations are added to this, the total is impressive. But atheism is not the exclusive possession of the communist world. Among intellectuals it is a live option. Among the Unitarian-Universalists one can find a good deal of atheism also. Among the philosophers in the universities atheism can be found in considerable numbers.

Among the existentialists, the words of Jean Paul Sartre sound the changes on the emptiness of life and its uselessness once man chooses the atheistic road. Sartre said: "Man can count on no one but himself; he is alone, abandoned on earth in the midst of his infinite responsibilities, without help, with no other aim than the one he sets for himself, with no other destiny than the one he forges for himself on this earth." As Francis Schaeffer has told us, this viewpoint has been widely articulated in modern music, painting, the movies, and philosophy.

In a sense, some people who claim to believe in God are worse off than the atheists. They are the ones who *act* as though they do not believe what they profess with their mouths. Is it not more tragic to deny in action what one professes by mouth, than to deny God and act the same way? True or practical atheism significantly influences the realm of ethics. Once a man denies God in principle, the ground on which to build any consistent ethical system is cut out from beneath him. The existence of God supposes ethical absolutes. Once these are destroyed, ethics is what one chooses for himself. Each man becomes the determiner of what his ethical standards will be. Marxist ethical outlook is consistent with its atheism. What the communist does is purely utilitarian, that is, whatever will help him reach the objective he has in mind is good. Thus for the Marxist to be a liar, a cheat, a covenant breaker, a murderer, a thief, an adulterer, or anything else is not only permissible but good. The system itself makes the doing of these things right. And since there is no cosmic judgment, no one to whom a final accounting is given in a transcendent sense, the holder of this view can do what he pleases.

The secularist and the communist or atheist think alike at this point. Because he does not acknowledge the existence of a sovereign God over all things, he becomes an ethical relativist. This attitude spills over into all areas of life. Whether one should be a fornicator, an adulterer, a breaker of his marriage covenant by divorce, a homosexual, a liar, a cheat in business, or a thief is based on the premise that he can do whatever he can get away with. The Judeo-Christian world and life view has been the glue which has held western society together. But that foundation has been rejected, and no adequate substitute for it has been found or will be found. For if any substitute simply reinforces what the discarded foundation supported, why discard the former foundation?

The conditions which exist within the professing church point to the second advent of Jesus, for the Church in the world has been secularized significantly. Blamires, in his book, *The Christian Mind*, says that there is no longer a Christian mind. Christians have been so brainwashed by secularism that they do not think like Christians. Their world and life view has its roots not so much in the Bible as in the agenda set by the world. Affluence, for example, is looked at in Scripture quite differently from the way the world and even the average Christian looks at it. A materialism based on possessions seems to have gripped the western world to such a degree that if the average Christian lost those possessions, he would, in all likelihood, lose his Christian faith as well. The Christian faith and materialism do not mix very well, and to the extent that materialism grips one's heart, to that extent his Christian faith has been diluted and sundered from its rightful base, which is spiritual and not materialistic.

Scripture does not say that believers are better Christians because they are poor. Nor does it say that material success is the hallmark of the good Christian life. Rather, it teaches that possessions must be looked upon as coming from the hand of God, and thus God is the author and the owner of all each one of us possesses. Ours is a stewardship of the God-given possessions, which are to be used under God's rules for stewards that they be found faithful. A simple life-style is the acme of stewardship, not the multiplication of possessions. Moreover, God requires of his stewards that they return to him tithes and offerings. It was David who said "All things come of thee, and of thine own have we given thee" (1 Chron. 29:14). All we can do is return to God a portion of what he has given us. And at death we surrender title to all we have for we go out the way we came in—empty-handed.

One reason why the Church has been secularized is that many of its people have lost their confidence in God. The Scripture does speak of apostasy, which is a falling away from the faith. It includes the deliberate rejection of revealed truth. Apostasy differs from error, which is usually the result of ignorance or the snare of the Devil. A person in error is not always to be counted an unbeliever, for true faith often is present in the hearts of some who entertain error. Apostates often continue to profess the Christian faith even while they deny by deliberate choice what they know has been revealed in Scripture by God.

What revealed truths, when denied, cut a man off from the true household of faith? Surely one of them is the denial of the deity of Jesus Christ, and another the denial of redemption through the atoning and redeeming sacrifice of Christ. These denials exist in many quarters in this generation. A new age of denial of Christ's deity seems to have come into the Church. This can be illustrated easily.

For years, the New Testament commentaries written by William Barclay, now deceased, have been read eagerly by ministers and laymen alike. They are probably the most widely sold set of commentaries on the New Testament today. Before his death, William Barclay wrote his autobiography. In that book he stated that Jesus Christ is not God, that the substitutionary atonement is untrue, that the virgin birth is not to be believed, and he went on to say that at last all men will be saved. His doctrine of the Holy Spirit was no better than his view of the person of Jesus. Although many people have been helped and blessed by some of the things he wrote in his commentaries, one thing remains clear: William Barclay was an apostate, and was not and could not be a member of the body of Christ, his Church, according to Scripture. Unless, of course, his universalism is correct, for in that event what one believes or disbelieves doesn't make any difference anyhow. Those who believe and those who disbelieve will get to heaven. It was Paul Tillich who said that he who denies God is by that fact affirming him and thus is saved.

John Hick, an English scholar, edited a book a year ago in which he and five other Oxford and Cambridge scholars contributed chapters (*The Myth of God Incarnate*, Westminster, 1977). Each author declared that Jesus Christ is not God. After the publication of the book, Hick received an appointment as a professor for a part of each year at the Claremont Graduate School in California. In an article interview of Dr. Hick by John Dart of the *Los Angeles Times*, it was reported that he believes salvation is to be found in any and all religions depending on your religious consciousness.

Robert Alley is a professor at a Baptist university, Richmond, in Virginia. He gave an address in a Unitarian church where he declared specifically that Jesus is not God. The president of the University of Richmond refused to fire him from the university because of freedom of speech, academic liberty, and tenure. Mary Picrone, a reporter from the *Richmond News Leader*, ran a series of articles in that paper after the Alley story hit the news pages of many papers. She quizzed professors all over America about their belief in Jesus as God. She learned that many professors do not think Jesus is God. All of them, however, make an outward profession of the Christian faith, but they are apostates. If one goes to Europe, the situation is no better. Today there is but one theological seminary in Germany that holds to the apostolic faith, and it was created recently. As a result of the erosion of belief in the theological schools, the churches have suffered greatly.

In western Europe, including Britain and Scandinavia, most of the churches are virtually empty. The lands where the Reformation was so successful have become mission fields which need the gospel preached to them once more. Church attendance in most of these countries ranges from two to five percent on Sunday mornings. Evangelism is dead and missionary outreach has shrunk dismally. Where the gospel is being preached, local congregations thrive, but they constitute a small minority.

In the United States, among the churches which are members of the National Council of Churches, there is not a single seminary of which it can be said that it is wholly orthodox and that its faculty is committed down to the last man as a believer in the deity of Christ and the substitutionary atonement of the Lord Jesus. Many of these churches have been losing members steadily and their missionary task forces overseas have shrunk. In a few years' time the United Methodist Church lost a million members; the United Presbyterian Church lost seven hundred thousand; the Christian Churches lost 563,000; the Protestant Episcopal Church lost 522,000; the United Church of Christ lost 211,000. The Division of Overseas Mission of the National Council of Churches reported approximately 12,500 missionaries some years ago. Today it numbers only approximately 5,000 missionaries with the constituency of around 38,000,000. Of the 5,000 missionaries, approximately 2300 come from agencies which are affiliated with the DOM but whose church bodies are not members of the NCC. The United Methodist Church has reduced its overseas task force by more than two-thirds. So has the United Presbyterian Church. These are all signs in America pointing to decline. The European situation has been grave for some years now. But what about places like Latin America where churches have been growing rapidly?

The Latin American situation is somewhat different from other parts of the world. The Roman Catholic Church has always claimed Latin America as its peculiar possession. Religious statisticians usually consider most of the people in Latin America to be Roman Catholic. If that were true, then substantial numbers of the Roman Catholics are leaving the church and becoming Pentecostals, independents, and others. Two things need to be said about Latin America. The first relates to the Roman Catholic Church.

Today, there are numbers of people within the Roman Catholic Church around the world who have come to a saving knowledge of Jesus Christ. Many of them choose to remain within that church for a variety of reasons. Some want to witness to relatives and friends about their new birth and feel that if they left the church they would not be able to do so. They remain within to be a light to those in darkness. Others worship in protestant churches and attend the Roman Catholic Church from time to time. But they find their religious sustenance in the protestant churches. They find it hard to leave the church of their childhood finally and irrevocably. But they no longer believe many of the doctrines taught by the church.

The Roman Catholic Church has been caught up in the same departure from the historic faith as have many protestant churches. It should be remembered that the Roman Catholic Church has always held to some of the important fundamentals of the Christian Church—the virgin birth, the deity of Christ, the Trinity, and the second advent. Their chief errors have centered around the mass, the Roman Church as the only door to salvation, baptismal regeneration, the immaculate conception, and the assumption of Mary into heaven in her body as well as the addition of tradition to the Bible as the foundation of faith, and the claim to infallibility of the pope.

A number of Roman Catholic scholars now accept the same liberal views as their liberal protestant colleagues. The Roman Catholics, however, were not the innovators who brought liberal higher criticism to the forefront. That was done by protestants. Johann Semler in the late eighteenth century taught at the University of Halle. He introduced the notion that Scripture and the Word of God are not synonymous. The Bible contains the Word of God but not all of the Bible is the Word of God. This opened the door to German liberal higher criticism, which called into question the basic historicity of the Old Testament. By the use of form criticism and the Wellhausen view, the Old Testament was reduced to a shambles.

In our generation, redaction criticism, which has risen out of higher liberal criticism and form criticism, has been applied to the New Testament. It has for its major premise the idea that the authors of the Gospels were writing theology, and in order to attain their purpose they put into the mouth of Jesus words he never spoke and assigned to him deeds or actions he never performed. They are still looking for the historical Jesus sought by Albert Schweitzer and other old-time liberals who never found him. Nor have the modern critics found him yet. Liberal scholars expect to gather together shortly to vote on which words of Jesus were really spoken by him and which were not; and which actions were his actions and which were attributed to him by Matthew, Mark, and Luke.

Roman Catholics have now been caught up in this same stream of liberal criticism. The Roman Catholic Church presently has in it scholars who are just as liberal as their protestant counterparts. They deny the virgin birth and the deity of Jesus Christ, too. The new Roman pope is fully aware of what is happening. And he has begun to crack down in an effort to bring back some semblance of theological unity to the church. He has rebuked Hans Küng, the German theologian and removed his name from the approved list of Roman Catholic teachers. He has rebuked Cardinal Schillebeeckx of the church in Holland. Hosts of scholars have risen up to defend these colleagues who stand outside the orthodox circle of the Roman Catholic faith.

The apostasy within the Roman Catholic Church is far worse and far more dangerous than that which characterized the church in the days of the Reformation. A cartoon in the *Los Angeles Times* recently showed the pope putting his finger in a leak in the theological dike. But it pictured a dozen other holes through which the water was leaking and no one was putting his finger in those holes to keep the church from sinking. Apostasy abounds in both the Roman Catholic Church and the protestant churches.

The second point which should be made about the Roman Catholic Church in Latin America and elsewhere is the increasing adherence by priests and people to the theology of liberation. In this instance, the theology of liberation seems to be a Roman Catholic contribution to the growing apostasy, a contribution which has influenced and affected the protestant churches around the world and especially the World Council of Churches. Gutierrez, a priest, has been the seminal father of the movement through his writings. At least in theory this cult (and it should be denominated as such) is based upon the desire to free the people of Latin America from oppression and social and economic injustice.

Gustave Gutierrez, in his novel book *A Theology of Liberation* (Maryknoll, N. Y.: Orbis, 1973) moves in the direction which will pave the way for the advent of the Antichrist. His theology is defective and his universalism causes him to concentrate his energies on socio-economic-political affairs to the exclusion of evangelization since all men are saved. He expresses an unqualified hatred for democratic capitalism and espouses socialism of the Marxist sort. He is wholly opposed to development, that is, the improving of the present economic situation. Instead he desires its overthrow and never bats an eyelash about the use of force to accomplish this goal. He covers it over with a Christian veneer that is in full agreement with the evolutionary temper of Pierre Teilhard de Chardin.

In his support of the Marxist view of history he wrote:

> It is necessary, therefore, to place in a single perspective the expansion of the developed nations. We must follow the new modalities very closely. These points were originally treated by authors such as Hobson and from another point of view by Rosa Luxemburg, Lenin, and Bukharin, who formulated the theory of imperialism and colonialism [p. 85, 86].

The Marxist idea of the class struggle as basic to the revolutionary process lies at the heart of his thesis. He said:

> But only a class analysis will enable us to see what is really involved in the opposition between oppressed countries and dominant peoples [p. 87].

The ultimate solution lies in socialism, for he said:

> Socialism, moreover, represents the most fruitful and far-reaching approach.... We must bring Indo-American socialism to life with our own reality, in our own language. This is a mission worthy of a new generation. According to Mariategui, Marxism is not "a body of principles which can be rigidly applied in the same way in all historical climates and all social latitudes...." Marxism, in each country, for each people, works and acts on the

situation, on the milieu, without overlooking any of its modalities [p. 90].

Gutierrez wants the destruction of the present system of capitalism, the end of the status quo. He exclaimed:

To support the social revolution means to abolish the present status quo and to attempt to replace it with a qualitatively different one; it means to build a just society based on new relationships of production; it means to attempt to put an end to the domination of some countries by others [what about Finland, Hungary, East Germany, Czechoslovakia, Lithuania and a host of other Russian satellite nations including Afghanistan?] The liberation of these countries, social classes and people undermines the very foundation of the present order; it is the greatest challenge of our times [p. 48].

On the mission of the Church Gutierrez stated:

In Latin America, the Church must place itself squarely within the process of revolution, amid the violence which is present in different ways. The Church's mission is defined practically and theoretically, pastorally and theologically in relation to this revolutionary process. That is, its mission is defined more by the political context than by intraecclesiastical problems [p. 138].

He proceeded to tie the mission of the Church to the universal salvation of all men with far-reaching consequences about the traditional view of that mission:

The questions raised by the notion of salvation have for a long time been considered under and limited by the classical question of the "salvation of the pagans." This is the quantitative, extensive aspect of salvation . . . . The evolution of the question has been complex and fatiguing. Today we can say that in a way this evolution has ended. The idea of the universality of the salvific will of God, clearly enunciated by Paul in his letter to Timothy, has been established. It has overcome the difficulties posed by various ways of understanding the mission of the Church and has attained definite acceptance [p. 150].

Gutierrez has in mind the ultimate goal for mankind—the creation of the *new man* under the aegis of a new system—socialism. He said:

Only a radical break from the status quo, that is, a profound transformation of the private property system, access to power of the exploited classes, and a social revolution that would break this dependence would allow for the change to a new society, a socialist society —or at least allow that such a society might be possible [p. 27].

It is important to keep in mind that beyond, or rather, through—the struggle against misery, injustice and exploitation the goal is the *creation of a new man* [p. 146].

The Latin American, by participating in his own liberation, gradually is taking hold of the reigns of his historical initiative and perceiving himself as master of his own destiny. Moreover, in the revolutionary struggle he is freeing himself in one way or another from the tutelage of an alienating religion which tends to support the status quo [p. 68].

At a deeper level, *liberation* can be applied to an understanding of history. Man is seen as assuming conscious responsibility for his own destiny [p. 36].

By way of conclusion, Gutierrez wrote:

Consequently, when we assert that man fulfills himself by continuing the work of creation by means of his labor, we are saying that he places himself, by this very fact, within an all-embracing salvific process. To work, to transform this world, is to become a man, and to build the human community it is also to save. Likewise, to struggle against misery and exploitation and to build a just society is already part of the saving action which is moving towards its complete fulfillment [p. 159].

By way of recapitulation, we can say that no one can dispute the claim that with a rapidly increasing population, Latin America suffers from great poverty. Nor can it be denied that the political situation and the ownership of most of the land by a small minority of the people have aggravated matters. The nations of Latin America have probably the worst record in the world for revolution. Regime after regime has fallen. But until recently, all the revolutions did was to change the control of each nation from one band of dictators to another while the masses of the people continued to be exploited. The encomienda system which came into being when the Spanish conquistadores controlled the continent was intrinsically evil. The Indians were enslaved by it. The system had the full support of the Roman Catholic Church. The combination of church and conquerors working together presented an impossible task for the Indians. They could not deliver themselves from their bondage. Moreover, Latin America never did have economic freedom. There was no democratic capitalism such as was to be found in the English settlements in North America.

Given the extremes of poverty and political powerlessness as well as social degradation, it is no wonder that the theology of liberation has been seen by the peasantry as their only hope for drastic changes to alter the balance of power and free them from their oppression. What they still do not know is that this cult is no better than the evil system under which they presently are governed.

At its heart, the theology of revolution is opposed to what it calls imperialism and capitalism. It looks with disfavor on America as though it is the agent of the status quo. This cult wants to destroy capitalism, which it thinks to be its greatest economic enemy. What the people fail to see is that they never enjoyed free enterprise at any time, nor do they realize that it was free enterprise or democratic capitalism which has given the West its economic advantage. They fail to see that the solution to their problem, as they seek to improve their standard of living is not to be found in socialism but in free enterprise.

The theology of liberation is strongly and unabashedly committed to socialism as the solution. In their understanding of the economic situation, the mentors of the theology of liberation have embraced the Marxist understanding of the historical processes. In theory at least, they have covered their socialism with a thin veneer of the Christian faith to make it palatable. Priests and nuns and even protestants who might be called evangelicals have been ensnared by this delusion. Shackled and oppressed, the masses hope that any change will bring them that freedom. But nowhere has socialism brought freedom. It has brought another form of slavery as witnessed by the experience in the Soviet Union, Red China, North Korea, Vietnam, Cuba and other nations.

José Miguez Bonino from the Argentine, unlike Gutierrez,

who is a Roman Catholic, is a protestant advocate of the theology of liberation. He gave a series of lectures at All Souls' Church, Langham Place, London. He wrote in his preface about his appreciation of the "sponsors of the London Lectures, and particularly to the chairman of the Board, the Reverend John Stott . . . I have not found in him or the other evangelical friends who have sponsored these lectures either dogmatic critics or accommodating flatterers but a group of deeply committed Christians trying seriously to come to grips, in the life of society, with the implications of their faith" [*Christians and Marxists, the Mutual Challenge to Revolution* (Grand Rapids: Eerdmans, 1976), p. 9].

Bonino said, "This book is written from the point of view of a person who confesses Jesus Christ as his Lord and Saviour" (p. 7). Then he spoke of his second presupposition:

A second presupposition belongs to the level of history: as a Latin American Christian I am convinced—with many other Latin Americans who have tried to understand the situation of our people and to place it in world perspective—that revolutionary action aimed at changing the basic economic, political, social and cultural structures and conditions of life is imperative today in the world. Ours is not a time for mere development but for basic and revolutionary change (which ought not to be equated necessarily with violence). The possibility for human life to remain human on our planet hangs on our ability to effect this change [pp. 7, 8].

Then came his third presupposition:

Still in another level lies the presupposition—which I shall try to argue throughout the book—that the socio-analytical tools, the historical horizon of interpretation, the insight into the dynamics of the social process and the revolutionary ethos and programme which Marxism has either received and appropriated or itself created are, however corrected or reinterpreted, indispensable for revolutionary change [p. 8].

Bonino heartily endorsed the statement made by Juan Rosales:

an Argentine Marxist author who has given careful attention—and much incisive criticism—to the role of religion in our society, makes this rather startling assertion:

"The bringing about of a true revolutionary transformation in our country . . . is for us [communists] *inconceivable* without the resolute participation of a renewed and engaged Christianity, which is equipped to make its specific contribution to the revolutionary baggage" [p. 15].

Latin Americans and foreign observers are equally arrested by this new phenomenon: not a Christian-Marxist dialogue but a growing and overt common participation in a revolutionary project, the basic lines of which are undoubtedly based on a Marxist analysis [p. 16].

Two characteristics of this relation should be immediately underlined. The first is that the relationship is quite lucid and conscious—at least among the leading participants. The Puerto Rico professor of theology Luis N. Rivera quotes with approval the remark of the Italian Waldensian Mario Miegge: "I *confess* that I am a Christian, but I *declare* myself a Marxist." This position, adds Rivera, represents that of many Latin American Christians "who find in Marxism a language of liberation adequate to articulate their revolutionary intention" . . . . "it should be inconceivable for progressive Christians" to envisage a revolution "without the orientating contribution of Marxism-Leninism or without the protagonistic activity of the working class" [p. 16].

Bonino goes on from there to endorse socialism (of the Marxist brand) and to damn capitalism. He dares to assert:

When we look at the history of socialist movements in this light, some facts acquire a theological significance. While Asia continues to be visited by the apocalyptic horseman called hunger, communist China has practically eliminated malnutrition, illiteracy and premature mortality for 800 million people in less than thirty years. While the Caribbean countries, constantly "helped" by the USA, continue to stumble from economic crisis to economic crisis, frequently in the grip of terror, instability and inflation, the island of Cuba, subjected to economic blockade, has been able to develop in less than twenty years the basis of prosperous agriculture and cattle raising, has established universal education and is beginning to develop new forms of political participation of the people in public life [p. 88].

This blatantly false statement is not the end of the matter. Bonino's unadulterated endorsement of Marxism from the Christian perspective permeates the entire book. His heroes are communists such as Ernesto (Ché) Guevara. He quotes from the writings of Ernst Bloch about "the red hero":

He confesses up to his death the cause for which he has lived and clearly, coldly, consciously, he advances towards that Nothingness in which he has learned to believe as a free spirit. His sacrifice is different from that of the ancient martyrs: these died almost without an exception with a prayer on their lips, confident that they had thus merited Heaven ... But the Communist hero, whether under the Tsars, under Hitler or under any other power, sacrifices himself without hope of resurrection. His Good Friday is not sweetened—much less absorbed —by any Easter Sunday, a Sunday in which he will personally return to life. The Heaven to which the martyrs raised their arms amidst flames and smoke, does not exist for the red materialist. And nevertheless he dies confessing a cause, and his superiority can only be compared with that of the very early Christians or of John the Baptist [pp. 135, 136].

Then Bonino draws this conclusion of his own:

Nobody who is acquainted with the tortures, the suffering, the death of thousands of communist revolutionaries —as we are today in Latin America—will want to retract or relativize a single word of this moving homage. "Greater love has no man than this, that a man lay down his life for his friends" (John 15:13) [p. 136].

Men like Bonino and Gutierrez are precursors of the coming Antichrist. However sincere may be their intentions, and however much they believe that Christianity and communism are blood brothers, they are molding world conditions to bring about a situation which will make it easy for the Antichrist to come to power and to rule over the earth. Synthesizing communism with Christianity when they are antithetical, and glossing over the resultant product with biblical verses about brotherhood will not change matters. It would be bad enough for the theology of liberation to find wide support in Latin America. But it now has gone far beyond Latin American borders to many other places around the globe and with similar consequences.

The theology of liberation, which has its roots in Latin America, has been exported to North America where it has penetrated the major denominations. It is getting more and more support among those who are related to the ecumenical movement. The World Council of Churches has been deeply influenced by it. The Fifth Assembly of the WCC which convened in Nairobi in 1975 displayed its ecclesiastical support, ranging from the Geneva hierarchy to numbers of the delegates from around the world. Men like Premier Manley of Jamaica were given platform visibility and his speech drew tremendous applause from the assembly. It was a thoroughly Marxist theology of liberation address. And his country since that time has been going downhill economically, not because of capitalistic imperialism but because of national socialism, which is bringing Jamaica to its knees economically. He continues, of course, to blame everyone and everything in sight except the system he advocates, which is the real cause of Jamaica's problems. Professor Robert McAfee Brown, who was then at Stanford University and who has gone to Union Theological Seminary in New York since then, was a featured speaker who embraced the same liberation line. It was he who more recently complimented Orbis Press, which is the Roman Catholic publishing house noted for its distribution of theology of liberation literature. He said he had come to see the light and the truth of the movement. Moreover, Union Theological Seminary is a hotbed for the advancement of this cult which is a substitute for the evangelism and missionary outreach the institution has lacked for years.

Moreover, the theology of liberation has a universalist twist to it. Since all men will be saved at last, the mission of the Church now becomes socio-economic-political in nature. Instead of saving souls they are now engaged in the business of saving society by the overthrow of the capitalistic system and the installation of Marxist socialism in its place. The agenda is a secular one, not a religious or spiritual one. There can be no doubt that the followers of liberation theology are stalking horses for the advance of Marxism-Leninism and great progress has been made. For a time, Chile fell under the dominion of the Marxists when Allende came into power. He decimated the country which is now only slowly recovering from the disasters it experienced.

It is not beyond the possibility that much of Latin America will come under the yoke of communism. And this continuing advance of communism around the world is one of the signs of the end times. In this instance, however, the advance is coming through the Christian church via apostates who by their promises of humanization and their insistence upon conscientization are making headway all over Latin America. The tragedy is that evangelical believers have not put together a world and life view so persuasive that it would be genuinely competitive to the Marxist-Leninist false utopia.

Those who are looking for the return of Christ should not sit on their hands as though nothing can be done and give the appearance of welcoming every adverse circumstance as another sign of the soon coming of the Lord. God has both his secret and his revealed will. His secret will keeps the time of his coming hidden from men except for general signs such as we have been elaborating. But these general signs have an element of mystery in them too. We can say with assurance that the description pictured by men like Harry Ironside, A. C. Gaebelein, C. I. Scofield and many others led them to think the second coming was upon them. They were wrong because they did not include the distinct possibility that there would be a further and deepening intensity of the signs they wrote about.

We who write about the second advent today must profit from the experience of those of other ages who looked for the soon coming of Christ. It is possible that there must be a greater intensification of all the signs we have talked about before the Lord returns. Things are bad, but they can get much worse. Only God himself knows what the intensity of evil must be like before the end comes. This means that there may be another interval of time longer than we have thought possible, and that Christ may not come for a hundred years. This should tell us that we must follow the revealed will of God, since we do not know the time of the coming of Christ which is in the secret will of the Father. It is the will of God for believers to strive against evil and to labor to improve the economic, political, and social conditions under which men live.

Socialism in its utopian and Marxist forms is a dead-end street which produces greater evils than those it intended to correct. Democratic capitalism is the only system which can actually do what socialism would like to do but cannot. This does not mean that democratic capitalism or free enterprise will have no evils attached to it. It is not the system which is at fault but evil men who misuse the system and who revolt against the revealed will of God, which includes ethical principles of stewardship and love one for another.

No system will deliver men finally from their distress and the dislocations of life rising out of original sin, but this does not mean that no effort should be made to improve world conditions. There are wrong solutions as well as right ones.

In his presidential electioneering efforts, Senator Ted Kennedy called for wage and price controls, something which is characteristic of socialistic systems. Innumerable economists have stated again and again that wage and price controls do not work. One, Arthur B. Laffer, professor of business economics at the University of Southern California, said in the Los Angeles Times, "The world record for wage and price controls from Roman Emperor Diocletian to the present is abysmal. It is equally bad on a company-by-company basis" (Feb. 7, 1980, II, 13). Men do not seem to learn from past experiences and so they repeat the mistakes over and over again.

Unfortunately, there are devout Christians whose commitment to utopian socialism is based on good hearts but simple heads without adequate economic learning. They preach about freedom in Christ in the spiritual realm, but they are the enemies of economic freedom. They fail to see that there are economic laws which are built into the universe in God's creation mandate just as there are physical laws, such as gravity. The breaking of God's economic laws is no less self-defeating than the breaking of his physical laws.

The theology of liberation with its Marxist view of history

and its promotion of socialism is another dead-end street. Its attractiveness, based on an appeal to the physical needs of the underprivileged and offering an unattainable utopian ideal which has never materialized, does have eschatological significance. Later we shall see that the advent of a world dictator will be brought about by an international desire for a pseudo-messiah who will offer men economic security and earthly provisions. Well may we live to see the day when multitudes will sing "I'd rather be Red than dead," and "I'd rather be fed with bread than worship the God who supplies bread for all men."

It is true that numbers of people are coming to a saving knowledge of Jesus Christ every year. We hear projections that Africa will be a Christian continent by A.D. 2000. Anyone who watched the Sixty Minutes television program when it focused on Liberia, which had for its governmental head a Baptist who has been president of the Baptist World Alliance, will see the flaw in the statement. One of his sons appeared in person and reflected a theology so far removed from historic Christianity, while professing to be a Baptist clergyman, that it was almost inconceivable. Since this was written Tolbert has been killed and his regime was overthrown by revolution.

If we total up all the people around the world, of whom it can be said that they are evangelical in their understanding of the Christian faith, they would represent a small minority of the world's population. When the views of many of the scholars among the churches of the world are looked into, it becomes apparent that they are far from orthodox. In many quarters, the theology of the Reformation has been lost, and the Roman Catholic and Eastern Orthodox churches are replete with priests and people who have no genuine attachment to biblical Christianity.

CONCLUSION

Many books have been written in the last hundred years about the second advent of Jesus Christ. All of them have alluded to the world conditions as a sign of the soon coming of the Lord. Obviously they all have been wrong for the Lord has not yet come. When we look at their evaluations of the times in which they lived and compare them with the times in which we live, we can draw one indisputable conclusion. The situation today is far graver and more closely resembles what the Scriptures describe than anything we have known for centuries. Perhaps there are worse times ahead, beyond what we have experienced, and the coming of the Lord must then await the worsening of the world situation. Surely there is nothing on the present horizon which would lead us to conclude that a new and wonderful age is dawning in which nations will live at peace and all men will enjoy prosperity. Anyone who entertains such a viewpoint does not derive it from the facts before us.

Pessimists do not receive the plaudits of the crowds, for nobody enjoys listening to those who paint dark and bleak pictures. The Scripture does paint a dark picture for us when it reveals the details of the end of the age. However it is realistic, not pessimistic. And the picture is always painted in such a way that the dark night yields to the bright day of hope and felicity. The darkness of the paradise lost is countered by the story of the paradise regained. There will be and there can be no paradise regained until man first comes to the end of his tether. He will have exhausted all options only to find himself at a dead-end street. There will be persecutions. There will be holocausts. There will be wars. There will be cosmic upheavals the like of which the world has never known.

The only question which remains is whether we are now entering into that age which will attend the end of history and the consummation of the age. Everything points in that direction. That is the least as well as all we can say. The coming of the Lord appears to be upon us when we look at the return of Israel to the land and the conditions of the world around us. And there is further evidence to which we must pay attention —the Arabs, oil, and the second advent of Jesus.

4

THE ARABS AND OIL A SIGN OF CHRIST'S COMING

THE MIDDLE EAST

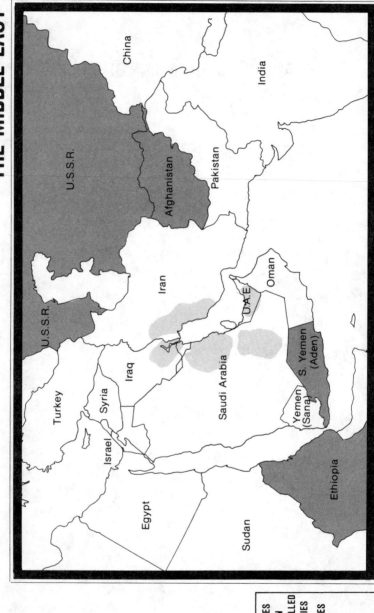

INDICATES RUSSIAN CONTROLLED COUNTRIES

INDICATES MAJOR OIL FIELDS

FOR TWELVE HUNDRED YEARS, THE ARABS HAVE NOT influenced the direction of the western world to any marked degree. The last Arab penetration of western Europe followed hard on the seventh century development of the Islamic faith by Muhammed. He was a successful caravan trader who claimed descent from Ishmael. He was born in A.D. 571 in Arabia. The people from whose loins he sprang regarded the city of Mecca as their holy place. Muhammed married a wealthy widow some years his senior. The beginning of Islam dated from what he thought was a vision from Allah, said to come through the auspices of the angel Gabriel. Muhammed wrote the Koran, which became the holy book of Islam. He claimed it was dictated to him by Allah from heaven. In 622, he made his famous hejira from Mecca, which had rejected him, to Medina, where he was greeted royally as an honored chief. Following this event, Islam became a dynamically religious movement, engaged in an offensive war which eventually threatened all of western Europe.

North Africa had been reached with the gospel of Jesus Christ during the first century A.D. It became a stronghold for the Christian faith. The famed city of Alexandria had one of the largest theological libraries of its day. When Islam moved westward, it eliminated the Christian faith as it took over North Africa, which has been under the sway of Islam ever since. The greatest defeat suffered by the Christian Church anywhere was registered in North Africa as a result of the Muslim incursion. The story is told that the famous library at Alexandria was destroyed after two questions were asked and answered: "Are the books in this library in disagreement with the Koran? If they are, destroy them because they will corrupt the true faith." The second question was, "Are these books in agreement with the Koran?" If the question was answered yes, the verdict was the same. "Destroy them, for they are superfluous."

So the entire library was burned to the ground.

The Arabs invaded western Europe, going into Spain. In A.D. 732, in the battle of Tours, the forward movement of the Arabs was halted decisively. It was not so much a result of defeat on the field of battle as it was the internal dissension in the Muslim dominions and a revolt of the Berbers in North Africa. From the eighth century onward until the twentieth, the Arab peoples played a minor role in world history. In the twentieth century, the Arab turnaround was brought about by one factor—the discovery of oil in Arab lands of the Middle East.

The Arab world comprises the peoples of North Africa and the Middle East. In North Africa, Morocco, Algeria, Libya, and Egypt are the major Muslim nations. In the Middle East, Syria, Iraq, Jordan, Saudi Arabia, Yemen, South Yemen, Oman, the United Arab Emirates, Qatar, Kuwait, Bahrain, Iran, and Afghanistan comprise the Muslim nations of the area. West Pakistan is Muslim, but it is geographically within the Indian area. The nations of the Middle East front on the Mediterranean, the Red Sea, the Persian Gulf, and the Arabian Sea, as well as the Indian Ocean. These Muslim nations number over 130 million people, most of whom are Arabs. Not all of the Arab peoples are directly descended from Ishmael. The Koran, the Muslim holy book and the Islamic faith is the glue which holds these diverse peoples together. Their major holy places of Mecca, Medina, and Jerusalem are of great importance to their faith. One reason why Jerusalem is the center of attention in world diplomacy is due to the fact that the Islamic holy place, the Dome of the Rock mosque, occupies the site where the Jewish temple, destroyed earlier by the Romans, is thought to have been located. The site is holy both to the Israelis and the Muslims. Arabs are permitted to visit the Dome of the Rock by the Israelis, who have stated boldly that the city is indivisible and will remain in their hands as long as time shall be.

It is true that oil is the key to an understanding of the role of the Middle East, but another factor is, and has been, important in the history of the region. The Russian czars and the Soviet communists, who succeeded them, have had a longstanding ambition to secure a warm water port for a nation whose major seaports are frozen over during the winter months. Long before the communists gained control of Russia, the czars sought to obtain a seaport on the Persian Gulf or the Arabian Sea. That desire did not disappear when the communists defeated the tsarist regime and brought Marxist socialism to the Soviet Union. Indeed, the importance of the Middle East has increased dramatically for several reasons. One has to do with the additional supplies of oil the Soviets will need during the 1980s. Another has to do with Soviet desire for world conquest.

The struggle between the communist bloc and the democracies in a major sense centers around the Middle East and its oil. The highly technocratic west and Japan are completely dependent on oil for their survival. In this sense, the Middle East oil nations have the west over a barrel, economically and politically. But the political aspect of the problem is perhaps the most important one of all. It is in the long range interest of the Soviet Union to destabilize the west and bring it to its knees. The control of the Middle East is essential to the Soviet plan for world domination. Thus, any consideration of the Arabs and oil must take into account the activity of the Soviets.

No one can refute the observations of Alexander Solzhenitsyn who, perhaps better than any other living man, speaks with authority about the inner workings of the Soviet Union and its intentions. In his commencement address given at Harvard University in 1978, he warned the West about its weakness and irresolution. His vision then was harsh and chilling, and it has not changed. He had earlier published *Warning to the West,* which is one of the most prescient books of this generation. After the Soviets swooped down on Afghanistan late in 1979, Solzhenitsyn wrote an article for *Time* magazine in which he reiterated his warning to the West about Soviet aspirations for world domination. He pointed out that there "is the prevailing, total incomprehension of the malevolent and unyielding nature of Communism, which is equally dangerous to *every* country." He went on to say:

> Try asking a malignant tumor what makes it grow. It simply cannot behave otherwise. The same is true for communism; driven by a malevolent and irrational instinct for world domination, it cannot help seizing ever more lands. Communism is something new, unprece-

dented in world history; it is fruitless to seek analogies. All warnings to the West about the pitiless and insatiable nature of Communist regimes have proved to be in vain because the acceptance of such a view would be too terrifying.

Solzhenitsyn piled word upon word as he spoke of the Soviet threat which of necessity has taken the Middle East into consideration as we shall see. He wrote:

Communism is unregenerate; it will always present a mortal danger to mankind. It is like an infection in the world's organism: it may lie dormant, but it will inevitably attack with a crippling disease. There is no help to be found in the illusion that certain countries possess an immunity to Communism: any country that is free today can be reduced to prostration and complete submission.

Then came the awful word of judgment about using the Chinese as a buffer to the Soviets. He said:

In expectation of World War III the West again seeks cover, and finds Communist China as an ally! This is another betrayal, not only of Taiwan, but of the entire oppressed Chinese people. Moreover, it is a mad, suicidal policy: having supplied billion-strong China with American arms, the West will defeat the U.S.S.R., but thereafter no force on earth will restrain Communist China from world conquest. . . .

Five years ago, all my warnings were ignored by official America. Your leaders are free to ignore my present predictions as well. But they too will come true [*Time*, Feb. 18, 1980].

A week before Solzhenitsyn's statement appeared in *Time* magazine the same publication printed Kissinger's *Warning of War*. This is what the *Time* article said:

The rhetorical question was whether the West faced "the prospects of a new war, not a cold one." And Henry Kissinger's answer to his own inquiry was grim indeed. "We must bring to a halt the Soviet geopolitical offensive," he declared last week. "It must be stopped even in the Soviet interest." If not, he said, the Western democracies may have to pay an even more fearful price than they did for failing to halt the rise of Hitler. Said

Kissinger: "In 1936 it would have been easy for the democracies to resist Hitler physically, but psychologically it was not. Five years later . . . they paid for their psychological uncertainty with 20 million lives."

The setting for this warning was the picturesque Swiss town of Davos, where a select group of European businessmen gather each year to discuss the future with distinguished guest speakers. A number of listeners were profoundly shocked by the former Secretary of State's message. Said one Austrian businessman: "Until hearing Kissinger tonight, I did not realize how profoundly the mood has changed in America. It will take us some time to catch up with that mood."

If Alexander Solzhenitsyn is correct in his analysis, and I think he is, several things become clear immediately. The first is that the Middle East is also on the expansionist calendar of the Soviets. They want, and will try, to take control of the Middle East. They covet the oil of this region for their own purposes, and they ardently desire to prevent the democracies from availing themselves of it. How important the oil is may be seen from the statistics. More than fifty percent of the known oil reserves are found in the Middle East. The United States has only five percent of the reserves. Western Europe and Japan are almost totally dependent on oil from the Middle East except for the North Sea supplies controlled by the British. Saudi Arabia is the biggest Middle East producer of oil. Iran, which is now in a state of disarray, has been the second largest producer. Kuwait, Iraq, the United Arab Emirates, Qatar, and Oman are small-time producers compared to Saudi Arabia and Iran.

The Soviet invasion of Afghanistan starkly signals what the communists are about. They are positioned so that they can attack Iran at will and gain not only oil fields but also a naval base or bases on the Persian Gulf. From this vantage point, they can wreak havoc on the movement of oil to Europe, America, and Japan. They can also descend on Pakistan from Afghanistan and move toward the Arabian Sea. Their influence in Yemen, and what they have done in Ethiopia, assures them of virtual control of the Red Sea and the passage through the Suez Canal. The stationing of a large navy in the Arabian

Sea area and the Indian Ocean would be of tremendous help to them in controlling the flow of oil around the South African cape, which is the only other way for oil to be shipped from the Middle East. Also the belt of communist-controlled nations north of South Africa and stretching from the Atlantic to the Indian Ocean gives them added leverage.

The Soviet master plan of world conquest of necessity calls for the elimination of the nonsocialist Middle East nations. They are capitalists who fall under the condemnation of Marxism-Leninism. They must be destroyed. Their destruction and takeover by the Soviets would be a windfall of unparalleled size. The oil nations of the Middle East have become the richest nations in the world. The OPEC combine, which they and other oil producing nations have brought into being, constitutes a monopoly. They can raise oil prices at will and bring the western democracies to their knees.

At the same time, as oil prices have been floating higher and higher, the American dollar has been losing ground steadily. The OPEC nations in some measure have indexed their oil prices to gold. As the dollar goes down, the price of gold goes up. As gold goes up, the dollar price for oil goes up with it. Inflation is about to bring the United States to its knees, but it is not caused by the increases in the price of oil. The wealth of the Middle East has increased so rapidly that the oil nations do not know what to do with it. They are buying into the banks, industries, farms, and real estate of the western nations and particularly the United States. They are accumulating gold reserves at an astonishing rate. They are providing their people with education, homes, and the luxuries of life. Little do they realize that as a result of this immense wealth they will bring grave problems to themselves and to their peoples. One can be sure that the Soviets will try to destabilize these nations for a later takeover. The more education the Middle East people obtain, the greater will be their disaffection and the more dangerous will be the possibilities for revolution and the overthrow of the existing regimes. The great caches of gold will also offer prize targets for enemy powers such as the Soviets, who themselves are in need of gold to cover their indebtedness to the West for their own overseas purchases.

Apart from Egypt, the Middle East has little or no affection for Israel. Surrounded on all sides except the West, Israel faces hostile Arabs who wish to bring about its downfall. The PLO has received considerable monetary support from other Arab nations which enables that organization to continue to be a thorn in Israel's side. It has consistently stated that it hopes to drive the Israelis into the sea. The PLO has used the United Nations, the Soviet Union, and the Arab states to attain its objective of a Palestinian state on the west bank of the Jordan River. Whatever may be the intrinsic merits of the Palestinians' case as a displaced people, it is plain that there is little hope of a peaceful settlement of the dispute. Neither side seems willing to budge.

From this data we can conclude that what has transpired in the Middle East in the last few decades was unthinkable a century ago. No novelist could have painted a picture which would have matched the reality in any way. With stunning suddenness, the backward nations of the region have come to life and have gained a power they never suspected could possibly be theirs. They can shake the chancelleries of the world. The mightiest nations wait with bated breath for the next rise in oil prices with the promise of OPEC that the prices will be adjusted every quarter from now on. Oil indeed has made the Middle East come alive. When the oil situation is looked at in the light of biblical prophecy, it should come as no surprise to Christians that this area of the world has assumed an importance undreamed of for centuries.

The Scriptures have foretold that the Middle East would be central to the events surrounding the second advent of Jesus Christ. The world's attention is fixed on this region and will remain fixed on it so long as oil for energy is essential to an industrial society. If the oil deposits were to disappear tomorrow, the Middle East would cease to be important. It would no longer enjoy a strategic role in international affairs. Therefore, we can conclude that the soon coming of the Lord Jesus is related to its geographic location and now especially the discovery and sale of oil in the Middle East. This is one of the key reasons why many students of eschatology think we are coming into, or are in, the beginning phases of the last days.

The Arab nations are using their newfound wealth in a frenzied manner to multiply their armaments. Their weapons could avail against lesser powers than the Soviet Union. But apart from Iraq and Iran, there is little chance that the Arab nations will fight each other. Israel is not going to start a war against the Arabs. She wants and needs peace to develop her industries, to balance her budget, and to reduce her inflation. Her adverse balance of payments constitutes a real problem and only continued financial help from the United States keeps her afloat. She is spending large sums of money on defense, for she knows fully well that a defenseless Israel would be a sitting duck for the PLO, Syria, and Iraq.

The major enemy of the Arab nations is the Soviet Union. She stands as a colossus whose military power exceeds that of any other power in that region of the world. The Soviets have developed all kinds of nuclear bombs, as well as delivery systems by which they can hit any target to which they direct them. Their navy is superior to that of the United States in some categories, and they outnumber the Americans in submarines, which prowl the seas even close to the U. S. mainland. A number of knowledgeable military leaders in the United States think the Soviets have a present capacity to destroy the American nation. Some observers think the Soviets expect the Americans will capitulate without the use of nuclear weapons. Instead of launching bombs, they will use nuclear blackmail, the threat of which will bring the United States to its knees.

The Scriptures nowhere clearly indicate what the role of America will be in the closing days of this present age. It is quite possible that it may become a second-rate nation of minor international significance before Christ comes. On the other hand, the United States is the largest consumer of oil and the best customer of the Arab nations. Its expertise in computer technology is the envy of the world. It still supports more missionaries than any other nation in the world. Its people are the source of immense sums of money not only for missionary purposes but for relief of the suffering peoples of the globe. It is likely to face its greatest economic challenge in the near future when it may have to change its currency, reduce its standard of living, and come to terms with its profligate habits. Solzhenitsyn and Kissinger feel that the West still can meet the Soviet challenge, but the former displays little hope that the leadership will pay any more attention to his analysis of the current situation than they did five years ago. He thinks the West is lethargic, self-centered, and soft. Solzhenitsyn's appraisal is lacking in one dimension. Up to this point he has not explicitly taken into account the oversight of God in the historical process, and for that reason he does not publicly offer the hope of deliverance from the present crisis by the coming of the Son of God in glory and great power.

The conjunction of a number of factors at this time frame of history enables Christians to hope that the coming dark days are only a prelude to the advent of Christ to consummate history. The Israelis are back in the land. The Soviet Union is at the height of its power. The oil-producing nations have risen to dizzy heights of influence through their economic clout brought about by the sale of oil. Advanced technology has made possible the instruments of destruction which can bring about the deluge described in the Bible. World economic, political, social, and religious conditions combine to flesh out the scenario for the coming of the Lord.

The Bible states that God promised to the descendants of Abraham the land "from the river of Egypt to the great river, the river Euphrates" (Gen. 15:18). "Every place on which the sole of your foot treads shall be yours; your territory shall be from the wilderness and Lebanon and from the River, the river Euphrates, to the western sea" (Deut. 11:24, RSV). This promise, which has never been fulfilled to date, includes a large area of the Middle East to the Euphrates River. How far south it is to extend the Scripture does not say. This is a fascinating promise at a time when the Arabs wish to eliminate Israel from any landed possessions in Palestine. It appears that Israel's gift of land from God goes far beyond the boundaries of Palestine and stretches over lands now in Arab hands where oil abounds and wealth is easy to come by.

How will Israel take this land from the Arabs when she has great difficulty keeping the small amount of land she now possesses? Will it come by war? And how would this relate to the promise of God that Assyria and Egypt will be at peace with Israel in the days ahead? If Gog and Magog refer to the Russian Bear as many believe, and if large armies will assemble at Armageddon for the final battle before the end of the age, how will the troops from Russia get to Palestine unless they move through Iran and Iraq and perhaps Turkey? Armies simply do not move through the territories of other nations unless there is a military alliance in which the armies of one nation move through the lands of other nations by agreement. The only other way for the Russian armies to move through these lands to get to Armageddon is to do so by conquering the lands through which they move.

In the last days, when the armies move to engage in battle at Armageddon, the Scriptures seem to say that Israel will be surrounded on all sides. There will be the coalition from the west which implies Rome. There will be a coalition of powers from the north which would be headed by Russia. The power from the south which will move toward Jerusalem seems to be Egypt which is presently at peace with Israel but which will later become Israel's enemy once again and send armies to destroy the nation. But there will also be the kings of the east, who will move through Arab lands to get to Armageddon. A great convulsion will follow. Israel will not be delivered by its own power and armaments. It will be delivered by divine intervention through the coming of God's anointed, the Lord Jesus.

One nation will not slay another nation in this final conflict. It will be God himself who will wreak vengeance on his enemies as he delivers Israel. So awful will this conflict be that there will be a river of blood 4½ to 5 feet deep. It will cover an area of two hundred miles which is the length of Palestine today. We can assume this means the whole land will be engaged in this battle from the north end, to the central section, to the south. The blood of the nations will be spilled over all the land. It would be imprudent for us to try to be minutely specific about the identification of all of these nations and armies. But of this we can be sure. The Arab nations will be caught up in this vortex and the singular position they occupy at this moment because of their oil will be theirs no more.

There is nothing in Scripture which indicates that Israel will take over the Arab lands which are part of God's promise to the Jews before the end of the age comes. Rather it seems that the fulfillment of the promise must await the coming of the Lord and the defeat of the enemies of God who are also the enemies of Israel. When we note tht the armies which are gathered at Armageddon come from the west, the north, the south, and the east, it leaves little room for the United States to be involved in this last great battle. Or Japan, for that matter. If the Roman Empire is rehabilitated it will, of course, involve western Europe. Since the Antichrist will rule over the whole planet, and since the United States is not mentioned in this last great battle, it may be that the United States will indeed, as we have intimated, become a second- or third-rate power of little significance, which would not be the case if a world war were to start today when the United States is still a first-rank power in the world.

This much we do know. The Arab or oil-producing nations are sitting in the middle of the world scene today and are exercising a power they have not enjoyed for centuries. They will continue to exercise this power so long as their oil is needed and they have control over these resources. And it appears that the end of the age must come upon us before the oil of the Arab nations has been exhausted. This could mean that the end is not far away and that the plan of God for the consummation of history will reach its climax in the not-too-distant future.

5

THE HEART OF THE STORM

THE SIGNS OF THE TIMES POINT TO THE END OF THE age. The Scriptures afford us some insights about what will happen during that period of time just prior to the second coming of the Lord Jesus in power and great glory with his saints and the angels of God. Three of the important happenings can be comprehended under the following titles: (1) The time of Jacob's trouble; (2) The tribulation; and (3) The Antichrist.

THE TIME OF JACOB'S TROUBLE

Modern Jewish history has been marked by the Holocaust, during which time six million Jews were destroyed in Hitler's concentration camps. As we have suggested earlier, the Jews who are alive today keep saying it will never happen again —there will never be another Holocaust. For those of us who take the Scriptures seriously and literally, there is every reason to expect that the Jews *will* suffer yet another holocaust before the second advent of the Lord Jesus. It will not come at the hands of Christians, for they also will be exposed to the persecution leveled against them by the Antichrist during the last days. Jews and Christians are going to be caught up in a cataclysm such as the world has never known.

The prophet Jeremiah (chapters 30-36) under the guidance of the Holy Spirit has given us some light on what will happen to the Jews in the last days. In verse 7 of chapter 30 Jeremiah said: "Alas! for that day is great, so that none is like it: it is even the time of Jacob's trouble, but he shall be saved out of it."

Jacob's trouble will be a time the like of which the Jews have never known. This is frightening when we survey the history of the Jews in the past. They suffered the loss of the ten tribes in the eighth century before Christ. The Southern Kingdom was overwhelmed and Jerusalem was destroyed under Nebuchadnezzar beginning in 586 B.C. the seventy-year-long Babylonian

Captivity. In A.D. 70, the Jews were massacred under Titus and Vespasian and those left were dispersed around the world. In Hitler's day they were massacred again when a substantial minority of all the known Jews in the world were murdered. But Jeremiah says that what the Jews still have to face will be worse than anything they have ever faced before. It will come when the world is under the aegis of the Antichrist, who will be the enemy of both the Jews and the Christians. There will be this difference, however. The Christians will suffer because they believe in, love, and follow Jesus. But the Jews will be in the land of Palestine in unbelief. Although, as the holocaust proceeds, multiplied numbers of them will come to know Jesus as their Messiah and in this sense will find deliverance even if they are killed.

Jeremiah says that this holocaust will come only after the Jews are back in the land of Palestine. He wrote: "I will bring again the captivity of my people Israel and Judah, saith the Lord: and I will return them to the land that I gave to their fathers, and they shall possess it" (Jer. 30:3). Many Jews are back in the land today. Scripture does not say how many of the known Jews in the world must be back in Palestine before this holocaust will take place. Therefore we must be careful not to suppose that the holocaust will take place immediately. It may be delayed until a greater number of the Jews have returned. At the same time, however, it may be that in the will of God the holocaust will take place on the basis of the number of Jews in the land at the present moment. And there is no reason to think that the Jews not in Palestine may not be part of a worldwide holocaust of this people.

If the word of this prophecy causes us to stagger in unbelief as to why God would let his chosen people suffer further indignities and awful death, we must remember that the secret will of God does not tell us all we would like to know as to the reasons why this shall come about. The ray of hope for the Jews comes in the last part of verse seven where Scripture says that "he shall be saved out of it." God will break the yoke of the oppressor. He will burst the bonds that bind his people Israel. They will come to know and serve God at last. He will be "the God of all the families of Israel, and they shall be my people" (31:1).

In the prophecy of Daniel, he mentioned Antiochus Epiphanes and predicted what he would do to Jerusalem and the temple. This prophecy was fulfilled in 168 B.C. But Antiochus Epiphanes is also a type of the final world dictator, the "beast" of Revelation who is yet to come. Antiochus is the type and the "beast" of Revelation is the antitype, and are called by the same name, the little horn. Antiochus Epiphanes was certainly a type of the Antichrist who is yet to come. He intended to force the Jewish people to surrender their religion, give up their ceremonies, and forsake their customs. He wanted to hellenize them, that is to press them into the Greek cultural mold and thus take away from them that which distinguished them from all of the other peoples of the world. Antiochus also sought to destroy the temple and replace it with one for the worship of the Greek god Zeus.

Antiochus did invade the Jewish temple and his soldiers entered the Holy of Holies. A pig was slain and its blood sprinkled on the altar and over the floor and the furniture of the temple. From the Jewish standpoint, no greater sin could have been committed. As if this were not enough, the priests were slain, the holy things of the temple removed, the worship of God and the reading from the Torah prohibited. Legally it became impossible for anyone to be a practicing Jew. Antiochus descended so low that he ordered the murder of the male Jewish infants who had been circumcised, and their mothers were forced to march down the streets with the corpses of their children hanging around their necks. In 164 B.C. the Maccabees succeeded in their revolt against the Hellenizers, a revolt which permitted a return of Jewish religious life and practices. To this day the Jews celebrate this event annually in what is labeled Hanukkah. God acted in this persecution, preventing Antiochus and his soldiers from completely destroying the people of God. This same God prevented Hitler from eradicating all of the Jews. And he will keep the Antichrist from doing so too.

Daniel said:

> In the latter part of their reign, when rebels have become completely wicked, a stern-faced king, a master of intrigue, will arise. He will become very strong, but not by his own power. He will cause astounding devastation

and will succeed in whatever he does. He will destroy
the mighty men and the holy people [Dan. 8:23, 24, NIV].
This description not only characterizes what happened in
Antiochus' day; it also will characterize the last days when the
Jews once more will face the weapons of destruction unleashed
in their midst. Daniel later expanded on his description of what
the end times will be like for the Jews. He wrote:

At the time of the end the king of the south shall attack
him; but the king of the north shall rush upon him like a
whirlwind, with chariots and horsemen, and with many
ships; and he shall come into countries, and shall over-
flow and pass through. He shall come into the glorious
land. And tens of thousands shall fall [Dan. 11:40, 41,
RSV].

The Antichrist, of whom Antiochus is the type, will be the
one in power at the end time. He will enter into a covenant with
the Jews which will last for the first half of the tribulation. At
the end of the three and a half years, there will be the World
War of all world wars. The Antichrist will go into Palestine.
Tens of thousands will be slain. The Antichrist "shall go forth
with great fury to exterminate and utterly destroy many" (Dan.
11:44, RSV). It will be a work of extermination—another holocaust.

Paul in Romans stated that God has not forgotten his people
Israel. Blindness has come upon them until the fullness of the
Gentiles has come to pass, and the Church of Jesus Christ has
taken in its last member, and the terms of the Great Commission have been fulfilled. The divine promise is that "all Israel
shall be saved: as it is written, There shall come out of Sion the
Deliverer, and shall turn away ungodliness from Jacob" (Rom.
11:25, 26). But the Scripture also says, "Who hath known the
mind of the Lord: or who hath been his counsellor?" God's
secret will is not known by men nor can it be. God will be God
and he will do what he pleases and when he pleases. Yet it was
Zechariah who stressed the awfulness of the last holocaust:

Behold a day of the Lord is coming, when the spoil taken
from you will be divided in the midst of you. For I will
gather all the nations against Jerusalem to battle, and the
city shall be taken and the houses plundered and the
women ravished; half of the city shall go into exile, but

the rest of the people shall not be cut off from the city [Zech. 14:1, 2].

Deliverance from the holocaust will not come from men but from God. Only divine intervention can save the Jews. That divine intervention will take place. Zechariah promised that "the Lord your God will come, and all the holy ones with him" (14:5). And "Jerusalem shall dwell in security" (14:11), something which is not true now, never has been true, and will not be true until the coming of Christ. The precariousness of the Jewish situation today is obvious to all. Inflation rages; the chief protector of Israel, the United States, seems to be edging away from that nation; Europe is doing nothing of significance to protect the State of Israel. The Jews themselves are highly divided into opposing parties and there is no clear-cut national unity of purpose or program.

One of the interesting signs of the times is the growth of the "Jews for Jesus" movement in the United States, where more Jews reside than in any other nation in the world. These converted Jews are sniped at and persecuted by their own people, who regard them as a positive danger to Judaism. Powerful Jewish agencies do all they can to cut off the labors of the Jews for Jesus. This Christian group of Jews is important for the future of Judaism, for it is through them and other converted Jews that the light of the gospel will come into historic Judaism and bring unbelieving Jews to the knowledge of Jesus Christ.

THE TRIBULATION

Just as there will be a final holocaust for the Jews, so will there be a holocaust for the people of God. This will occur during the period denominated in Scripture as the tribulation. It is that period of seven years just prior to the second advent of Jesus Christ. It is the seventieth week mentioned in Daniel's prophecy of the seventy weeks (Dan. 9). It will be divided into two parts: the first half of the tribulation will witness the wrath of man poured out on all the earth.

As the tribulation begins, an apostate Christendom in the form of a worldwide ecumenical church of a syncretistic sort will think it is doing the world a favor by helping the Antichrist's rise to world power. The Antichrist will destroy the ecumenical church, demand to be worshiped as God, force all people to receive the mark of the beast, and fashion a covenant with Israel which will last for the first half of the tribulation.

The persecution which comes from the Antichrist against the Christians is poured out because they worship God; the wrath of the Antichrist which is poured out against the Jews will come at a time when they have not yet received Jesus as their Messiah. But the persecution against them will bring them at last to acknowledge Christ as Messiah and be saved. God thus uses the wrath of man to accomplish his purposes for his believing people.

The second half of the tribulation, generally called the great tribulation, will witness the outpouring of the wrath of God even as the wrath of man continues. One of the important questions has to do with the relationship of the Church to the whole of the tribulation period. This will be considered later when we talk about whether the Church will go through the tribulation or any part of it. For the moment, we only need to remember that during this period multitudes of Gentiles will be converted, will either be martyred, or will go through this awful experience. Who they are, and what provision is made for them, will be discussed later on.

Jesus talked about the course of this age. He mentioned wars and rumors of wars. He spoke of famines, pestilences, and earthquakes. He prophesied there would be hatred, false prophets, and betrayals. In some measure, all of these things have come to pass and have characterized history for the past two thousand years. But they will greatly increase in extent and intensity as the end of the age reaches its climax. Jesus promised that "then shall be great tribulation, such as was not since the beginning of the world to this time, nor ever shall be" (Matt. 24:21). In other words, the tribulation period will make all periods of history seem tame by comparison. When we recall the slaughter of multiplied millions of people by the Soviet Union and Red China, these evils will be minor compared to what will happen in the last period of human history.

During the tribulation, large numbers of Jews and Gentiles will turn to Christ for salvation. Revelation 7:4-8 speaks of a Jewish remnant and records the number as 144,000 out of all the tribes of Israel. The same chapter mentions the multitudes of Gentiles who come to Christ as well. It says:

> After this I beheld, and, lo, a great multitude, which no man could number of all nations, and kindreds, and people, and tongues, stood before the throne, and before the Lamb, clothed with white robes, and palms in their hands .... What are these which are arrayed in white robes? and whence came they? ... These are they which came out of great tribulation, and have washed their robes, and made them white in the blood of the Lamb.... They shall hunger no more, neither thirst any more ... and God shall wipe away all tears from their eyes [Rev. 7:9, 13, 14, 16, 17].

This Scripture provides us with data which should be noted carefully: (1) great multitudes will be saved, which can only mean that the gospel will be preached one way or another during the tribulation and the Holy Spirit will convict, convert, and regenerate those who trust in the Lord Jesus; (2) great numbers of the redeemed will witness to their salvation by the shedding of their blood—they will be martyred for the sake of Jesus and for their testimony; (3) they will have suffered hunger and thirst and their eyes will have shed countless tears —but after their martyrdom, they will enjoy the fountains of everlasting water and God will wipe all tears from their eyes. Surely terrible times will come, but the saints of God will receive at last the peace of God and divine provision for their every need. Thus, there will be a holocaust during the great tribulation for the saints who come to know Jesus Christ even as there will be a holocaust for the Jews. The Scripture which says "there is no difference between Jew and Gentile—the same Lord is Lord of all and richly blesses all who call upon him (Rom. 10:12, NIV) will be fulfilled. Who, then, will bring the convulsions which will rock this earth and who will pour out the full measure of human wrath on the planet Earth before and during the time when God will pour out his divine wrath for the three-and-a-half-year period just prior to the battle of Armageddon and the personal, visible, and triumphant coming of the Son of God?

THE ANTICHRIST

The Word of God says that there will be many antichrists during the course of this age (1 John 2:18). John is very specific about what the antichrists and the future Antichrist will be like. All of them are marked by their denial of Jesus. John says:

Who is a liar but he that denieth that Jesus is the Christ? He is antichrist that denieth the Father and the Son. Whosoever denieth the Son the same hath not the Father: [but] he that acknowledgeth the Son hath the Father also [1 John 2:22, 23].

Always and ever, the Word of God is called into question, the Written Word and the Incarnate Word. In a manner far beyond any denial of Jesus before the period of the tribulation, the end of the age will be characterized by the greatest denials of Jesus as God, and the Bible as the trustworthy Word of God. Whoever denies that Jesus is God cannot know or have the Father. Salvation cannot come to those who deny Jesus. They are apostates if once they apparently professed the faith; they are tares which wait their commitment to the lake of fire if they never acknowledged Jesus as Savior and Lord.

Throughout the history of the Christian Church, there have been unbelievers and apostates. Cult after cult have arisen which have denied Jesus Christ as he is revealed in the Holy Scriptures. Unitarianism is one of the worst instances of apostasy in western Christendom. In the United States, New England experienced the great Unitarian defection in the nineteenth century. A large number of the Congregational churches of that area were lost to the historic faith. When these churches became Unitarian, they still clung to some aspects of the heritage which was theirs from Congregationalism. But gradually they lost even those good aspects of their inheritance.

Today Unitarianism is spiritually bankrupt in a complete sense. Some of its leading lights are secularists, and numbers of them are no longer theists. Once the deity of Jesus Christ is lost, men and institutions quickly plunge deeper and deeper into apostasy and move farther and farther away from anything which remotely resembles the true faith of the apostles and prophets.

One of the most amazing phenomena is that local councils of churches around the United States include Unitarian-Universalist churches and their ministers in their membership. This is even stranger since the National Council of Churches has never admitted the Unitarian-Universalist churches into its membership; nor does the World Council of Churches. There would be just as cogent reasons to admit Christian Science churches, or Jehovah's Witnesses assemblies, or Mormon stakes as there is to admit Unitarians. Such is the state of affairs these days.

The antichrists of which the Scriptures speak are bad enough. The individual called *the* Antichrist sums up in his person all of the evils of all the antichrists who have ever appeared on the scene of history. He will have incorporated into his person every conceivable evil; he will exceed in his wicked actions all that the worst men known to history have ever done. In his person, Satan will be virtually incarnate. This is the final phase of the war which has been fought in the seen and unseen world between God and Satan and his hosts of darkness across the ages. It will be Satan's last demonic effort to defeat the purposes of God. So he will rally all his cohorts, combine all the efforts of evil men, and bring together the greatest combination of the powers of darkness ever to have appeared on the planet Earth.

John reveals that the titanic struggle for cosmic control will be waged in the heavens as well as on earth. He says that "Michael and his angels fought against the dragon; and the dragon fought and his angels, and prevailed not; neither was their place found any more in heaven. And the great dragon was cast out, that old serpent, called the Devil, and Satan, which deceiveth the whole world: he was cast out into the earth, and his angels were cast out with him" (Rev. 12:7-9). Then a word of warning is spoken to the earth dwellers: "Woe to the inhabiters of the earth and of the sea! for the devil is come down unto you, having great wrath, because he knoweth that he hath but a short time" (Rev. 12:12). The Antichrist will be the tool of Satan to do his work and to seek to accomplish his malign purpose, which is the defeat of Jesus Christ. Moreover, the Scripture says that in this struggle when Satan has come to earth, men can overcome him only "by the blood of the Lamb, and by the word of their testimony; *and they loved not their lives unto the death*" (Rev. 12:11, italics mine).

The Antichrist will be the last world dictator. In the Word of God, a number of different titles are applied to him. He is called the beast in Revelation 11:7 and 13:1. He is the lawless one of 2 Thessalonians 2:3. He is the spoiler (Isa. 16:4), the prince that shall come (Dan. 9:26), the little horn (Dan. 7:8), the vile person (Dan. 11:21), and many others.

The Antichrist will be a person of intense convictions. He will not pussyfoot around nor will he pretend to be what he is not once he has gained power. He will have great power and he will use it unsparingly. Just as Adolph Hitler stated his intentions in *Mein Kampf* for all the world to read, so the Antichrist will reveal his intentions once he has consolidated his power. He will fear no one and will parade before all as the supreme ruler of the world. He will force every knee to bow before him as though he is God, or he will dispose of them in his own holocaust, which will exceed in numbers and terror anything Hitler ever did.

What will be his program, what will he stand for, or perhaps we should say, what will he be against? First, we can be assured that this world dictator will come. Many antichrists have come and gone, but this one called the Antichrist will come. He will be a person, not simply a force or some occult power. He will be a human being with supernatural powers at his disposal which he will employ freely. He will oppose Jesus Christ and his teachings. He will not allow that Jesus is even an option but will strike at the Son of God in his person and his relationship to the Father. He will laugh at his atoning sacrifice on the Cross of Calvary. He will go beyond Jesus and make light of God the Father. This will be a denial of the God of history. He will be, in a technical sense, an atheist. But in the practical sense, he will not be an atheist for he will set himself up as God. The Caesars did this under the title of the Pontifex Maximus.

What title the Antichrist will give himself and what claims he will make will be aimed at the destruction of the God of the Scriptures. He will deny that Jesus, the second person of the Trinity, has come in the flesh. That is, he will deny the Incarnation which lies at the heart of God's redemption. He will also laugh at the Lordship of Christ. He will do two things: he will oppose Jesus and all he stands for; but he will also take the place of Christ and claim to be all that Jesus was, whose claims he will say are untrue. Thus he will be the great deceiver.

The Antichrist will come, as it were, from the bottomless pit to exalt himself and to demand that he be admired and worshiped by men. Arrogant, fearless, and a liar, he will come to destroy, not to heal, and he will engage in his work of iniquity. A law unto himself, this son of perdition will do as he pleases, but God will bring him down to hell and cast him into the lake which burns with fire. He will wage ceaseless war against Jesus according to Rev. 19:19 (see also 17:14).

We are not to imagine that the Antichrist will be a dolt, an ignoramus, or one lacking in gifts. He will "come in peaceably, and obtain the kingdom by flatteries" (Dan. 11:21). He will use all the stratagems necessary to gain his dictatorship. He will appear so attractive to men who seek for deliverance from international troubles that they will happily see him enthroned as a dictator who will promise what he cannot and does not intend to deliver. He will use the religions of the world in such a way that leaders of religion everywhere will get behind him. The ecclesiastical establishments will "give their kingdom unto the beast, until the words of God shall be fulfilled" (Rev. 17:17).

The Antichrist will be a charismatic person in that he will be a persuasive orator with a "mouth speaking great things" (Dan. 7:8). Revelation 13:5 says that "there was given unto him a mouth speaking great things and blasphemies ... and he opened his mouth in blasphemy against God, to blaspheme his name, and his tabernacle, and them that dwell in heaven." He will not be modest in his opinion of himself either. He will, says Daniel, "exalt himself, and magnify himself above every god" (Dan. 11:36). He will be an intelligent, shrewd, skilled, and persuasive politician. The leaders of the nations would not give their allegiance to a dunce. He will have the abilities to discharge the functions of his office as dictator. Satan himself will recognize his gifts and abilities, for he will give him "his power and his seat, and great authority" (Rev. 13:2). He will appoint wicked men to high office to aid him in his war against God. The "false prophet" of Rev. 13:11-17 will be an able and helpful assistant, who will be his minister of propaganda.

The Antichrist may well be a Jew. Daniel says, "Neither shall he regard the God of his fathers" (Dan. 11:37). Perhaps even as Jesus the Messiah was a Jew, so also his antitype, the Antichrist, will also be a Jew. He will attack Christians furiously, for the Scripture says: "And it was given unto him to make war with the saints and to overcome them; and power was given him over all kindreds and tongues, and nations" (Rev. 13:7). He will not bring peace but a sword to the world, and the saints of God will be among those who experience the holocaust.

The true children of God will feel the sting of the Antichrist's persecution. Many of them will die. But God will grant them strength in the hour of their trial. He has told them that he who overcomes "will I grant to sit with me in my throne, even as I also overcame and am set down with my Father in his throne" (Rev. 3:21). Multitudes of believers will have to face this choice: the Antichrist or God. Reduced to its simplest components, it will be God versus Satan, light versus darkness, heaven versus hell; the New Jerusalem versus the lake of fire.

6

THE ANY-MOMENT RAPTURE OF THE CHURCH

WHEN WILL THE CHURCH BE RAPTURED? THAT IS THE sixty-four dollar question. Surely no one who takes the Bible seriously and literally will deny there is a rapture. Paul in First Thessalonians teaches this so patently that we must accept the fact and try as best we can to understand it in the light of all the events which comprise the end times. For those who say the Church will go through the tribulation, the rapture, time-wise, can only take place at the same time, or a very short time before the glorious appearing of the Lord Jesus himself on this earth. For them, then, the rapture is preceded by known, recognizable, and predicted events which must come to pass before the Church is caught away.

A host of believers agree that the Church will be raptured before the seven-year period generally called the tribulation of which the great tribulation takes place the last half of the seven-year period. Many, if not most, of the pretribulational rapturists hold that the event can take place at any time. It is to this viewpoint, and to the people who hold this view, that the question must be addressed: Is the rapture of the Church an event that could have taken place any time after Pentecost when the Church first came into being? It is possible, of course, for those who believe the rapture can occur at any time now to hold that it could not have happened earlier. All the predicted events needing to be fulfilled before the rapture have indeed come to pass. Thus the rapture can *now* take place at any time. A great host of pretribulational rapturists, however, seem to be saying that the event in question could have happened any time during the church age.

Leaving aside the question whether the rapture can *now* occur at any time and assuming that no predicted prophecies remain to be fulfilled before it happens, we will consider the question whether Jesus could have come again at any time after the Church began at Pentecost. It must be said immediately that

Jesus could not have come at the very least before the twentieth century. Stated another way, there were known and predicted events which had to take place before the Lord could rapture the Church. We will look at the biblical evidences which substantiate this statement. Then we will show that a number of the best-known pretribulation rapturists said the same thing at least by implication and that some were quite inconsistent by seeming to say things which were antithetical to each other.

BIBLICAL DATA AGAINST
AN ANY-MOMENT RAPTURE IN BYGONE DAYS

In Luke 21:24, Jesus said that "Jerusalem shall be trodden down of the Gentiles until the times of the Gentiles be fulfilled." Two important points are contained in this prophecy: (1) Jerusalem, which was then in the hands of the Jews, would be wrested from them and controlled by the Gentiles; (2) the control of Jerusalem would last until the "times of the Gentiles be fulfilled."

Jerusalem was seized from the Jews under Titus and Vespasian in A.D. 70. This was some years after the resurrection of Jesus and after the Church had begun at Pentecost. Christ could not have returned before this event happened unless the prophecy was not meant to be fulfilled. That would be impossible. This one prophecy by itself invalidates the notion of an any-moment rapture after Pentecost. One might argue that he could have come any time *after* A.D. 70, but this is also impossible from the biblical data.

The Jews, as we have seen, are now back in the land, and Jerusalem once more is under their control. In the short 1967 war, the Jews passed through the Mandelbaum Gate which separated the old Jerusalem from the new city and took over the ancient section of Jerusalem. From that day to this, the Gentiles have not had control of the city. It is useless to suppose that this is not the fulfillment of Jesus' prophecy recorded in Luke's gospel. The possibility that Jerusalem will be taken away from the Jews again and later come under their control before the end times has no support from Scripture. Nowhere does the Bible suggest that Jerusalem will be taken from the Jews twice. We should not construct charts to fit preconceived notions. None of us was or is on God's program committee for setting up the events connected with the end of the age.

The return of the Jews to Jerusalem is, in itself, a compelling reason for us to say that Jesus could not have returned to this earth until this prophetic event took place. Good men may have supposed that Gentile ascendancy over Jerusalem would cease *after* the rapture, not before. And certainly we ought not to claim that Scripture explicitly states, when this event was predicted in the Bible, that the rapture would come after the return to Jerusalem. But we know that this has happened. Its having happened makes clear that since the Church has not been raptured, the event had to take place prior to the rapture. We can understand and excuse earlier earnest students of the Word who were wrong about this matter. But we have further light and can see now that those who held to an any-moment rapture were incorrect in their interpretation of Scripture.

A third reason why an any-moment rapture is an impossibility is related to the Great Commission and the Church. It is true that dispensationalists who hold to a pretribulational rapture say the Jews will finish the work of world evangelization after the rapture of the Church and when the Holy Spirit has been withdrawn. C. I. Scofield says (p. 1343) that what he calls the everlasting gospel "is to be preached to the earthdwellers at the very end of the great tribulation and immediately preceding the judgment of the nations (Matt. 25:31, refs.). It is neither the gospel of the kingdom, nor of grace. Though its burden is judgment and not salvation, it is good news to Israel and to those who, during the tribulation, have been saved (Rev. 7:9-14; Luke 21:28; Ps. 96:11-13; Isa. 35:4-10)."

The Great Commission as given in the Acts of the Apostles just prior to Christ's ascension into heaven was directed to the Church and not to Israel. The disciples were present then and also when they were given the commission to evangelize the world as recorded in Luke's Gospel. In the Lukan account, they were commanded to wait in Jerusalem for the promise of the Father which was the coming of the Holy Spirit whose power they needed to help them. This refers to Pentecost. Then, in Acts, Jesus says to the same disciples who will constitute the Church at Pentecost: "But ye shall receive power, after that the

Holy Ghost is come upon you: and ye shall be witnesses unto me both in Jerusalem, and in all Judaea, and in Samaria, and unto the uttermost part of the earth" (Acts 1:8).

This statement of the Great Commission was not only a command; it was also a promise. It says they *shall be* witnesses unto the uttermost part of the earth. The rapture of the Church, therefore, had to await the fulfillment of that prophecy and that command to take the gospel to the ends of the earth. At the opening of the nineteenth century, that commission had by no means been fulfilled yet. Christ would not come and the Church would not be raptured until that commission had been fulfilled. And as long as the rapture does not take place we know that the Church is to be busy finishing the task of world evangelization.

We must now scan the writings of some of the great expositors on the subject of the rapture who have been identified as holding to an any-moment rapture of the Church from the earliest times as a possibility. Harry A. Ironside is the first example.

HARRY A. IRONSIDE

Dr. Ironside was the pastor of the famed Moody Church in Chicago. He was a splendid preacher and Bible teacher as well as an able writer. In 1915 he wrote a book titled *The Midnight Cry*, which centered around the soon coming of the Lord for the Church. In the preface to the 1928 revision he wrote:

> So rapid have been the changes, and so markedly has the way been prepared for the predicted end of the age ... that it has been thought wise to bring it more nearly up-to-date by adding considerable new matter and making a few revisions. None of the latter have in the slightest degree modified the views originally set forth, as every passing year has but convinced the writer of the certainty of the prophetic program revealed in the Word of God and *confirmed by the signs of the times* [my italics].

Obviously that which is "confirmed by the signs of the times" cannot be something which was confirmed in all of the earlier ages, for then the signs would mean nothing. Instead, Dr. Ironside found, in his day, something different from other ages which led him to conclude that the rapture was around the corner. This is further confirmed by what he wrote later on:

> The apostolic band and believers in the earliest period were all looking for His return. Yet He came not, and long centuries have since elapsed. What evidence is there that *now* His advent is so nigh, and that there may not be as long a time to elapse ere He comes back than has already passed? . . . What can be gleaned from the past history of, and present conditions prevailing in the Church of God that would indicate the soon closing-up of the present age and the coming of the Lord Jesus Christ? [pp. 10, 11].

Later Dr. Ironside said things even more specific which indicate how wrong one can be when concluding that the time of the rapture is at hand:

> But now that nearly twenty centuries (two of God's great "days"—2 Peter 3:8) have elapsed, we can look back over the long course of the Church's pilgrimage and see how all her varied states and experiences were foreknown and foretold and the heart thrills with joyful expectancy as we look ahead. For the *next* [my italics] miraculous event *must* be the shining forth of the Morning Star, the coming of the Lord Jesus, and our gathering together unto Him [p. 12].

Dr. Ironside did not live long enough to see the passing of the control of the city of Jerusalem from Arab to Jewish hands. He evidently believed the Church would be raptured before that event took place. He was wrong. Even more clearly he said with passionate urgency:

> Reader, let me press my point again.—The world-wide Gospel proclamation and world-wide apostasy *at the same time* are clear proofs that the end is close upon us. [p. 28].

But since we know that neither of those conditions had existed in any previous age of the Church's history, the Lord could not have come for his Church until they did exist. Dr. Ironside was saying that *now* the time was ripe and what had never been true before was true when he wrote. Furthermore, he did what we shall see Dr. Scofield did too. He identified the messages to the seven churches as portraying seven periods in the Church's history of which the Laodicean age is the last. He said:

> Laodicea is the closing period of the Church's history, and who can doubt that we have now reached the very time predicted? It behooves us to act as men who wait for their Lord, knowing that His coming cannot be much longer delayed [p. 35].

Is it not clear that the Church could not have been raptured until the Laodicean age was reached? Dr. Ironside called the Laodicean age the "closing period of the Church's history." How then could there have been an any-moment rapture when he knew that the Church had to go through six prior ages before the arrival of the Laodicean age?

Dr. Ironside said "the apostolic band and believers in the earliest period were all looking for His return." Does the Scripture say this in the sense he understood it? Hardly. What is more important is whether we who have come after them have read into the biblical account of the last days some things which may not truly represent what they had in mind when they were speaking about the coming of the Lord. Of this, we shall have more to say a bit later.

C. I. SCOFIELD

The Scofield Bible has had a long and honored ministry for almost three quarters of a century. Cast in the dispensational tradition, it has been "the Bible" for hundreds of thousands of believers. The Scofield notes have suckled several generations of Christians and have provided them with a systematized theology on a more popular level. Before the copyright expired, a revised Scofield Bible was issued by the Oxford Press and included in its list of revisers men like E. Schuyler English, Wilbur M. Smith, Frank Gaebelein, and John Walvoord. Some of the Scofield notes were changed considerably in the revision, with the view to correcting internal discrepancies.

Curiously, the original Scofield Bible does not list the rapture of the Church in the index at the end of the Bible. Nor is it listed under Church. In the note for 1 Thessalonians 4:17, C. I. Scofield did not use the word "rapture." He wrote: "Not church saints only, but all bodies of the saved, of whatever dispensation, are included in the first resurrection as here described, but it is peculiarly the "blessed hope" of the Church. . . ." This note was changed in the revised Scofield. Moreover he denominated the rapture of the Church as the first resurrection but when he footnoted Revelation 20:6 which speaks specifically of the first resurrection he did not connect it with the rapture. How there can be two first resurrections remains for later consideration.

When speaking of the Day of the Lord the Scofield Bible says it is preceded by seven signs: "The sending of Elijah . . . cosmical disturbances . . . the insensibility of the professing church . . . the apostasy of the professing church, then become Laodicea . . . the rapture of the true church . . . the apocalyptic judgments and . . . "the 'day of God,' earth purged by fire" (p. 1349). Since Elijah has not yet come, it appears that this is one of the prophetic signs which yet remains to be fulfilled once Dr. Scofield placed the rapture after the appearance of Elijah. Thus he could not hold to an any-moment coming for the Church from the earliest day. (The new Scofield Bible has altered this footnote.)

Dr. Scofield also adopted the same view of the messages to the seven churches as Dr. Ironside. He wrote:

> Most conclusively of all, these messages do present an exact foreview of the *spiritual* history of the church, and in this precise order. Ephesus gives the general state at the date of the writing; Smyrna, the period of the great persecutions; Pergamos, the church settled down in the world, 'where Satan's throne is,' after the conversion of Constantine, say, A.D. 316. Thyatira is the Papacy, developed out of the Pergamos state . . . . Sardis is the Protestant Reformation, whose works were not 'fulfilled.' Philadelphia is whatever bears clear testimony to the Word and the Name in the time of self-satisfied profession represented by Laodicea [p. 1332].

In the outline for Laodicea, Scofield called it "the final state of apostasy." Thus it is evident that the seven churches represent seven periods of church history of which Laodicea is the last. This obviously means that there could not have been an any-moment rapture of the Church until the church age was finished.

ARNO C. GAEBELEIN

Arno C. Gaebelein is listed as one of the consulting editors for the Scofield Bible. He wrote a book, *Things to Come* (N.Y., n.d., "Our Hope" Publication Office). It comprised four lectures on prophecy. Dr. Gaebelein, like Drs. Ironside and Scofield, could not logically hold to an any-moment rapture of the Church from the days of the apostles. In his book he spoke about certain predictions of things to come taken from the New Testament. He said the predictions are grouped around six things: (1) Denial of the faith; (2) Denial of sound doctrine; (3) Denial of the power of godliness and therefore unholy living; (4) Denial that Jesus is come in the flesh; (5) Denial of the Lord himself; (6) Denial of authority. The conclusion he drew from this list is that at no earlier time in the history of the Church have these things been true. So he wrote:

> And now we come to the most solemn fact. *We behold about us the complete fulfillment of all these predictions.* Not one of them is unfulfilled. It is true in the past there have been false teachers, departures from the faith and delusive teachings, but never before has the fulfillment of these predictions been so intense, so persistent, so widespread as in our days. Nothing more remains to be fulfilled. . . .
>
> *Again we say it is a most significant fact that we behold about us the literal fulfillment of all these predictions concerning the last days. What an evidence this is that the Bible is the Word of God* . . . The next great event is *nothing less than the Coming of the Lord for His Saints* [pp. 8 ff., italics mine].

In fairness to Dr. Gaebelein, it should be said that he believed in the any-moment coming of Christ for his Church at the time he wrote his book. It is also clear that he could not have believed in an any-moment rapture of the Church from the days of the apostles. He said there were predictions which had to be fulfilled. He said these predictions had been fulfilled. He said that the next event in the order of things was the rapture of the Church. Like Dr. Ironside and Dr. Scofield, he did not know of the return of the Jews to Palestine, and of the end of Gentile ascendancy over Jerusalem. Thus he was wrong in concluding that all the prophecies requiring fulfillment before the rapture had indeed taken place. And while some of us may think we have come to that moment when nothing more remains to be fulfilled before the rapture, the experience of these men should teach us to be undogmatic about this.

MARTIN R. DEHAAN

Dr. DeHaan was the featured speaker on the Radio Bible Class program for many years before his death. He enjoyed a magnificent ministry, was thoroughly orthodox in the Christian faith, and was a strong defender of that faith. He was a firm believer in the imminent coming of the Lord for his Church. Again the question arises whether he believed that the imminence of Christ's coming was taught and believed from the beginning of the Church age, or whether he held that all of the prophetic events needing to be fulfilled before the rapture of the Church was possible had taken place. His writings show clearly that he could not have held to the imminence of Christ's coming from the earliest days. This conclusion derives from his own statements which indicate that many prophecies had to be fulfilled before the Lord could come for the Church. If he did hold to imminence from the earliest days, he was simply inconsistent and was unaware of that inconsistency.

In his book *Coming Events in Prophecy* (Grand Rapids: Zondervan, 1962) he spoke about the course of this age. He said:

> In Matthew 13 Jesus teaches His disciples by the use of seven parables of the Kingdom the characteristics of this present age of mystery.... While all of the parables describe the general condition of professing Christendom during this entire dispensation, *they also represent seven successive periods of Church history* [my italics].... Today the first six historic periods of Church history are almost completed. We are now in that period of the hidden treasure and the precious pearl. Within the past few decades more prophecies concerning Israel, God's treasure, have been fulfilled than during the past nineteen hundred years [pp. 93-95].

In connection with Daniel's prophecy Dr. DeHaan wrote:

> In Daniel 12:4 we read: "But thou, O Daniel, shut up the

127

•

words, and seal the book, even to the time of the end:
many shall run to and fro, and knowledge shall be increased."

The meaning of Daniel's words could not be understood until they actually came to pass, and that would be
at the time of the end. Up until this present generation
we could not understand what Daniel meant by the
words, "many shall run to and fro, and knowledge shall
be increased." They were sealed until the time of the end.
Today we know what Daniel meant—there is no doubt
about it any more; and so we know it is the time of the end
[my italics]. What an accurate description of today we
have in the phrase, "many shall run to and fro, and
knowledge shall be increased" [p. 101].

These extracts show unmistakably that Dr. DeHaan could
not consistently hold to an any-moment rapture prior to the
writing of his book. There were prophetic events which had to
be fulfilled before the rapture could occur. There were, he said,
seven successive periods of Church history; that is, one period
followed another. This meant that Christ could not come for
the Church until the six periods of Church history had taken
place. In his statement from Daniel's prophecy, Dr. DeHaan
says that Daniel's prophecy was sealed until the time of the
end. Now it has been unsealed and we know it. "It is," he says,
"the time of the end." Clearly, then, until this took place Christ
could not return for his Church. So an any-moment rapture
from Pentecost onward was an impossibility. This does not
mean, of course, that Dr. DeHaan may not have been saying
that the time when an any-moment rapture could take place
has come upon us now.

Dr. DeHaan did raise an important question about the relationship between a belief in the imminent coming of the Lord
and spirituality and evangelistic activity. He said:

Show me a man or a church or an assembly which truly
believes in the personal imminent return of Christ at any
moment, and I will show you a man or an assembly that is
spiritually on fire, striving for holiness, ablaze with zeal
for souls, and fired with the spirit of evangelism [p. 40].

And then later on he wrote:

Anything which destroys the imminency, the possibility

of His any-moment return, robs us of that blessed hope, for the greatest incentive to holiness and evangelism and soul-winning and service *throughout* [my italics] the history of the Church has always been the blessed promise of His Word, "Because thou hast kept the word of my patience, I also will keep thee from the hour of temptation, which shall come upon all the world, to try them that dwell upon the earth" (Revelation 3:10). And only thus can the words of our Lord mean anything at all when He says, "Watch, therefore, for ye know not what hour your Lord doth come" [p. 132].

Since Dr. DeHaan's own statements indicate that he could not consistently have held to an any-moment rapture until this present age (the time in which he was writing), then this puzzler remains: Did men like Augustine, Calvin, Luther, Wesley, Edwards, and thousands of others lack "spirituality on fire," a "striving for holiness," and were they lacking in evangelistic zeal and were they not "ablaze for souls"? And did the fact that there were prophecies which had to be fulfilled before the rapture of the Church "rob [them] of that blessed hope"?

Earl D. Radmacher, a confirmed and ardent pretribulation rapturist who stands for a signless time for the event to take place, had this to say about getting believers into spiritual living because the rapture may be close upon us. He wrote:

Great discredit to prophecy has been brought over the years and today by those who, even with proper motivation, seek to use "the signs of the time" to bring believers into line, so to speak. I find that I can identify very much with Robert Mounce when he says: "This approach seems to say that what is really important is to be in good shape at the particular point in time when Christ returns. (It's the old I-don't-want-to-be-caught-in-there-when-Jesus-returns syndrome). It suggests in a veiled way that the mark we get on our ethical report card is the mark we happen to receive on the pop quiz given at the Parousia rather than the cumulative grade for the entire course." ["What If It Were Today," *Eternity*, February, 1974.]

Surely we can look for that blessed hope and the glorious appearing of Jesus Christ, even if it is still a thousand years away. Surely we are not to determine how we shall live on the basis of the nearness or the farness of the coming of Christ. We are called to be faithful regardless of these things. And yet there is a great truth contained in the warning about watching for the coming of the Lord. Christ will come for each one of us one way or another. He either will come in his second advent or he will come for us in death when our days on this earth are over and we can work no more. Those of us who believe in the imminence of the Lord's coming should be at work with zeal and commitment, but we should work this way even if we thought his coming was to be delayed beyond our lifetimes.

I. M. HALDEMAN

I. M. Haldeman, pastor of the First Baptist Church in New York City, was a great preacher and a fervent believer in the any-moment coming of the Lord. His writings indicate that he also could not have consistently maintained that the any-moment coming of the Lord was held and taught in Scripture from the earliest times.

Like the others quoted here, Haldeman said that certain prophetic events foretold in Scripture had to be fulfilled before the rapture of the Church was possible. His book *The Signs of the Times* was written to show that the time for the coming of the Lord was upon us and he proved it from the signs of the times. But if these signs were common to all ages, that would have meant nothing new had come. It would simply have been a rehash of what was old. But Dr. Haldeman spoke of new things which had never transpired before which were signs to him that the coming of the Lord was now upon us.

Among the news events which convinced Dr. Haldeman that the coming of the Lord was now imminent had to do with the Jews. In the preface to the eighth edition of his book he said:

> The Jew is back in Palestine. He is there under a mandate from the League of Nations, and that mandate delivered and sustained, as foretold by England, who backs it with her army and navy—"the ships of Tarshish."
>
> They are returning to the homeland by the thousands every month and, as the prophets foresaw, in a state of

intensified unbelief . . . . The desert is "blossoming as the rose" [p. v].

By so much, then, as the Zionist movement is a climactic sign and witness in these times that the day of the Lord is at hand, by just so much it is a witness that "at any moment" the "door of heaven" may be opened, the Lord may speak, and all those who own his name be bidden to rise and meet him, see him face to face, and share his glory. This is the deeper meaning of Zionism [p. 366].

The Jew had been out of the land of Palestine for almost two thousand years when Dr. Haldeman wrote this. Now they were coming back. And he regarded it as a necessary prerequisite before the Lord could come. His any-moment coming was based upon the fulfillment of what Dr. Haldeman believed to be all of the prophetic Scriptures that had to be fulfilled before the coming of the Lord. So he promoted an any-moment coming at his point in history because the signs of the times which had not come to pass in earlier history had now been fulfilled.

Dr. Haldeman supplied many other evidences to support his thesis that the soon coming of the Lord as evidenced by fulfilled prophecies was upon us. He did not know when he wrote the book that the Jews would wrest Jerusalem from the Arabs before the rapture, but he would surely have included that among the fulfilled prophecies indicating the soon coming of Christ. So we must repeat once more that the return of Jerusalem to Jewish control is one of the clearest signs that an any-moment rapture of the Church could not have occurred until this event took place.

JOHN WALVOORD

Dr. John Walvoord, the president of Dallas Theological Seminary which was founded by Louis Sperry Chafer, is a keen student, scholar, and teacher of the dispensational viewpoint, which generally has included in its system a belief in the pretribulational rapture of the Church. There are dispensationalists today who do think the Church will go through all or at least part of the tribulation period. Dr. Walvoord is not one of them. He holds firmly to the pretribulational viewpoint. Later we will discuss the time of the rapture. In that regard the question is whether Dr. Walvoord holds to an any-moment rapture of the Church because all predicted prophecies which had to be fulfilled before the rapture could take place have now been fulfilled; or that there could have been an any-moment rapture from Pentecost onward. It is here that Dr. Walvoord appears to be inconsistent. He does appear to commit himself firmly to the view that the rapture was imminent from the earliest days. Then he goes on from there to speak of signs which nullify imminence as he holds it. He wrote:

ARE THERE SIGNS OF THE LORD'S RETURN?

When the rapture of the church was explained, no signs were ever given indicating the specific expectation of that event . . . This attitude characterized the early church, which believed that Christ could come at any day. This has been the hope of the church from the first century until now. Any suggestion or theory which implies that Christ could not come today is not what has been commonly believed through the centuries [*Armageddon*, (Grand Rapids: Zondervan, 1975), p. 198].

At this point we must introduce the evidence connected with the writings of Dr. Earl D. Radmacher, president of the Western Conservative Baptist Seminary of Portland, Oregon. He is a Dallas Theological Seminary graduate, possesses an analytical mind and is a strong defender of the pretribulational rapture. In his tract *Signs of a Signless Event?* (Western Baptist Press, 1976) Dr. Radmacher is keenly aware of the fact that so many of the pretribulationists who hold to a doctrine of imminence also talk about signs in connection with the event. He holds that this is a gross inconsistency. He wrote:

Nowhere does the Scripture place any necessary action or event before the rapture [p. 7]. In answer to Oswald Allis, therefore, I would admit that there is a glaring inconsistency in those who preach about the signs of a signless event. *There are no signs of the times because we are not in the time of the signs* [p. 8].

Then Dr. Radmacher went on to say:

I realize that some will respond by saying that prophetic fulfillments cast their shadows before them and that, although there are no prophecies to be fulfilled before the rapture, there are after the rapture. The weakness of this argument, however, is that we have no idea of the length of the time period between the rapture and the first prophesied event, the manifestation of the Antichrist [p. 8].

Dr. Radmacher and Dr. Walvoord are fully agreed that the rapture is a signless event. As we shall see, however, Dr. Walvoord falls into the trap Dr. Radmacher mentions. He does employ "signs" whether he uses the word or not. They appear in principle in his book on *Armageddon*. Dr. Radmacher is conscious of a inbuilt problem in his signless position. Thus he allows for some time to pass between the moment the rapture occurs and when the Antichrist establishes his covenant with Israel which marks the beginning of the Day of the Lord.

In order for the Antichrist to sign a covenant with Israel, Israel must be back in the land and in control of Jerusalem. Until recently, however, Israel has not been back in the land and at no time until this generation could it be said that Israel had control of the city of Jerusalem. Dr. Radmacher knows fully well that Israel must be back in Palestine at the end times, and of necessity this is a sign of the rapture which must occur before the end times according to pretribulationism. And he knows that if Israel is not in the land when the rapture occurs, it would take some time for her to return and to take over the city of Jerusalem. So he solves this problem by introducing an unspecified time period between the rapture and the Day of the Lord. Very few pretribulationists hold to this view.

If the rapture had occurred a thousand years ago, as Dr. Radmacher says it could have, we would still be waiting for the rise of the Antichrist. And if Israel were not in the land and Jerusalem not in her control, it would be something which would not happen in a short space of time. Dr. Radmacher and Dr. Walvoord both have the same problem. They offer opposing solutions, both of which create further problems. Dr. Radmacher is correct in saying that men like Dr. Walvoord are logically inconsistent. Dr. Radmacher, on the other hand, introduces a view which is logically consistent but practically mind-boggling. Unless he can point to biblical evidence showing that the time interval between the rapture and the beginning of the Day of the Lord is quite short, he has opened the door wide to a time period of indefinite length (for he openly confesses "we have no idea of the length of the time period between the rapture and . . . the manifestation of the Antichrist") which could mean a thousand or ten thousand years. The whole tenor of Scripture links the rapture and the end times so closely together that Dr. Radmacher's case seems hopeless. It would be far simpler for men like Dr. Walvoord to say they are mistaken in their understanding of Scripture with regard to the rapture as signless in any meaningful way.

In the case of Dr. Walvoord, the book he wrote in conjunction with his son shows that he (they) do exactly what Dr. Radmacher opposes. They make statements which can only be interpreted as denying an any-moment rapture from the days of the apostles. Dr. Walvoord wrote:

THE PROPHETIC PULSE OF JERUSALEM

The prophecies about Jerusalem make it clear that the holy city will be in the center of world events in the end time . . . In our present rapidly moving world scene with the Middle East once again becoming the center of the stage, it becomes dramatically clear that these events may not be too far distant. . . .

As *signs* [my italics] that we may be moving into this period multiply, the direction of present world events also points to the conclusion that the coming of Christ for His Church, promised in John 14, may occur any day [*Armageddon*, pp. 96, 97].

Especially significant is Dr. Walvoord's statement:

Prophecies about Israel, and especially Jerusalem, provide important reference points for all of prophecy. The most significant prophetic event in the twentieth century has been the restoration of Israel. All the prophecies of the end of the age indicate that at that time the Jews will be back in their land and in precisely the same situation in which they find themselves today.

All areas of prophecy combine in the united testimony

that history is preparing our generation for the end of the age. In each area of prophecy a chronological check-list of important prophetic events can be compiled. In each list in regard to the church, the nations, or Israel, the events of history clearly indicate that the world is poised and ready for the rapture of the church and the beginning of the countdown to Armageddon [*Armageddon*, pp. 199, 200].

Dr. Walvoord provided what he termed "A Prophetic Checklist for the Church." He said:

This checklist includes the major prophetic events *in the order of their predicted fulfillment* [my italics].

1. The rise of world communism marks the new beginning of the politics of atheism.

2. Liberalism undermines the spiritual vitality of the church in Europe and eventually America.

3. The movement toward a super-church begins with the ecumenical movement.

4. Apostasy and open denial of biblical truth is evident in the church.

5. Moral chaos becomes more and more evident because of the complete departure from Christian morality.

6. The sweep of spiritism, the occult, and belief in demons begins to prepare the world for Satan's final hour.

7. Jerusalem becomes a center of religious controversy for Arabs and Christians, while Jews of the world plan to make the city an active center for Judaism.

8. True believers disappear from the earth to join Christ in heaven at the rapture of the church.

And then he went on to add numbers 9 through 13 which are not relevant to this discussion of the any-moment rapture of the Church.

Dr. Walvoord's approval of imminency from the days of the apostles is in conflict with the statements I have just quoted. The two viewpoints are apparently opposed to each other.

How do we resolve what appears to be a contradiction? The contradiction is this: Scripture appears to accept in principle what it denies when it speaks of prophecies which must be fulfilled before the rapture takes place. And this becomes Dr.

Walvoord's problem as well. Jesus specifically foretold the destruction of Jerusalem and it happened as he foretold it. This brute fact took place in A.D. 70. Jesus had not yet come, and the day of the Lord had not yet begun. Were the apostles wrong in holding to the imminency of the Lord's return, or have we misunderstood what they had in mind? Moreover, Christ said the Church would be witnesses unto him to the ends of the earth in Acts 1:8. This had to take time and Jesus could not have returned for the Church until his own prophecy about the Church was fulfilled. The Jews have taken Jerusalem. This fulfillment of Jesus' prophecy came almost two thousand years after it was uttered. Either we must disclaim this as a fulfillment of the particular prophecy or agree that the rapture of the Church is indeed preceded by the fulfillment of certain prophecies. If the latter judgment is correct, then an any-moment rapture from the days of the apostles cannot stand.

It is always possible to argue that had the apostles known then what we know now, the situation would be different. Even if this were so, we must insist on the principle that Scripture cannot contradict Scripture, whether the authors knew or didn't know what we know today by way of fulfilled prophecy. Moreover, the Holy Spirit is the divine author of the Word of God and he knows the end from the beginning. Therefore, we must conclude that the early church's attitude toward the coming of the Lord was something other than that understood by those who hold to imminence. Dr. Walvoord said that:

> The detailed development of pretribulational truth during the past few centuries does not prove that the doctrine is new or novel. Its development is similar to that of other major doctrines in the history of the church[The Rapture Question, p. 192].

Assuming this to be so, we must still insist that any early or late development of any truth cannot contradict any Scripture.

To look for the coming of the Lord to rapture the Church does not in itself imply imminency. I look forward and have looked forward to being with Jesus Christ at death. I have waited more than sixty years for what has not yet happened. I can wait during my lifetime with expectancy for the future coming of Christ, whether it is soon or will come a thousand years from now. Scripture says that Simeon was waiting for the consolation of Israel (Luke 2:25). The Holy Spirit assured him that Jesus would come in his day (Luke 2:26). But the prophecy of the first advent of Jesus began with the prediction in Genesis 3:15. Many people were waiting for that first coming of the Lord. They waited for thousands of years. And a thousand years are as a day in the sight of God. Jesus did not come and he could not have come until the fulness of time. And Daniel's prophecy of that first advent pinpointed the time. But this did not keep the people from looking for the coming of Jesus the first time, even though they waited for approximately six hundred years after Daniel's prophecy.

Every premillennial scholar agrees that specific signs, giving detailed information about events which will transpire during the tribulation period, are found in Scripture. The overwhelming verdict of those who hold to a pretribulation rapture is that this so-called "signless event" is followed immediately by the seven-year tribulation period. Thus, immediately following the rapture of the Church, Israel and the Antichrist will enter into a covenant. "Three-and-a-half years before the second coming of Christ," says Dr. Walvoord, "the dictator in the Mediterranean will desecrate a future Jewish temple and stop the sacrificial worship of God being carried on in this temple" (Armageddon, p. 95). The obvious is all too apparent. There could be no rapture until the Jews come back to Palestine and Jerusalem is in their hands so they can rebuild the temple. This rebuilding of the temple could not take place unless Israel was in the land and in control of old Jerusalem unless the rapture occurs an indefinite period of time before the Day of the Lord commences. The Jews must be in the land before the tribulation begins. The Jews are in the land, although the rapture has not yet taken place. Thus, it becomes plain that the signs having to do with the tribulation are pertinent to the rapture and that these signs make an any-moment rapture from the days of the apostles an invalid thesis.

CONCLUSION

In conclusion, the following statements may be made about the any-moment rapture of the Church:

1. The predictions about events taking place during the

tribulation period, events which have been fulfilled by way of preparation, make an any-moment rapture of the Church from the day of the apostles invalid.

2. It is possible for us to speak of Christ's imminent coming in this generation even though the word imminent is not found in Scripture *per se*. We can conclude that his coming looks to be likely during the next three or four decades. But this must be a tentative conclusion, since others who preceded us were certain of his earlier return and were proved to be wrong. It may be that a longer period of time than we presently envisage may be necessary to prepare the scenario for the tribulation period.

3. We have closed the door to imminency from the days of the apostles, but we have left open without discussion what may be the most important question in the minds of multitudes who think the Lord is coming shortly. The question is this: Will the Church go through the tribulation, or will it be raptured before the tribulation begins, or during the middle of that terrible time? We cannot dodge this question, and to it we must now address ourselves.

7

WILL THE CHURCH GO THROUGH THE TRIBULATION?

THE QUESTION, "WILL THE CHURCH GO THROUGH THE Tribulation?" may well be one of the most widely discussed, if not the most widely discussed subject in the area of eschatology (the doctrine of the last things). Some of those who believe that the Church will be raptured before the tribulation hold this view on the basis of their own wish to escape the awful calamities which will overtake the world. Thus, for some of them, the pretribulational view does not derive so much from their careful study of the Scriptures as from their personal desires. This attitude is understandable because most people, if the choice were left to them, would prefer to be taken out of the world before the time of Jacob's trouble, the appearance of the Antichrist, and the outpouring both of the wrath of man and the wrath of God.

We must remember that, in the final analysis, none of us is on the divine program committee, planning the events of the end times, and all of us are closed up to Scripture for our opinions on the time of the rapture of the Church and all the other items in our theology. In some matters Scripture is plain. No one can deny, for example, that the virgin birth is taught in Scripture. No one has to believe in the virgin birth even though it is taught. But disbelief means a denial of what Scripture clearly teaches. When it comes to the mode of baptism and the subjects of baptism, the Scripture is not so explicit. And may it not be that when Scripture treats the time of the rapture, it may not be explicit? Perhaps the only correct answer to the question of the time of the rapture is hidden in the secret will of God and is not part of the revealed will of God.

THE TIME OF THE RAPTURE NOT EXPLICIT

Again and again we have stated that Scripture says explicitly that there will be a rapture of the Church. We also have stated that the viewpoint represented in this book is that of premillennialism. We know that some people embrace the amillennial position and a few are postmillennialists. I do not know of any amillennialists or any postmillennialists who say the Church will not go through the period of the tribulation. Among premillennialists, some say the Church will be raptured before the tribulation period begins, others say the Church will be raptured in the middle of the tribulation period, and some say the Church will be raptured at the end of the tribulation period.

To the best of my knowledge no evangelical says that any particular position on this subject must be held in order to be a Christian. Virtually all Christians refuse to make pretribulationism, midtribulationism, or posttribulationism a test of fellowship. Moreover, none of the well-known confessions of faith constructed by protestant churches through the ages takes a stand on the time of the rapture of the Church. In fact, the pretribulational viewpoint seems to have come into the Church only in the last several centuries. We must hasten to add that this does not, by reason of that fact, mean that it cannot be a correct viewpoint.

In past centuries, many books on systematic theology popularized the postmillennial viewpoint, a doctrine which is not now held in high esteem by most biblical scholars in the evangelical tradition. Indeed even though premillennialism can be shown to have existed in the Church through the ages, it is only in the past several centuries that it has become widely held by Christians.

Once we agree that the time of the rapture should not divide believers, we can go on to observe that two of the resolute defenders of pretribulationism and posttribulationism state that neither view is explicitly taught in the Word of God. John Walvoord, the president of Dallas Theological Seminary, is one of the strongest advocates of dispensational pretribulationism. In his book *The Rapture Question*, he wrote:

> Ladd . . .[who is the strong defender of posttribulationism] concedes that [the] posttribulational rapture is an inference rather than an explicit revelation of Scripture in the following statement: "Nor does the Word explicitly

place the Rapture at the end of the Tribulation." The fact is that neither posttribulationism nor pretribulationism is an explicit teaching of Scripture. The Bible does not in so many words state either.

May we not conclude, then, that since the Bible is not explicit about the timing of the rapture, this area should not be a matter over which there should be division? But when we have said this, we still are obliged to take a hard look at the data of Scripture to see if we can, for good reasons, lean in one direction or the other. What evidences can we adduce from the Bible to throw light on this difficult question?

THE DAY OF THE LORD

When discussing the pretribulation rapture, the phrase "the Day of the Lord" has important implications. Depending on the meaning of the phrase, different conclusions can be arrived at. John Walvoord, in his important book *The Rapture Question*, acknowledges that what he calls "the older pretribulationists" or the "early pretribulationists" were mistaken in their understanding of that phrase. They "identified the Day of the Lord with the millennium and placed its beginning at the return of Christ to establish His earthly kingdom, an interpretation later popularized by the Scofield Reference Bible." By so doing, they endangered the view of imminence because instead of the coming being unexpected and unannounced, it could be virtually dated since "it would be preceded by such events as the great tribulation and other notable signs." Moreover "it jeopardized their teaching that the translation of the church was uniquely an event unheralded and imminent." Dr. Walvoord notes that this confusion enabled posttribulationists to strike back.

Two points should be noted here. First, Dr. Walvoord rightly observes that pretribulationism is of recent origin. He speaks of the "early pretribulationists" by which statement he virtually affirms that the view was not at all common to the period of church history preceding the Brethren writers with whom it originated. Secondly, he is saying that the view of these early writers about the meaning of the "Day of the Lord" undermined their case decidedly. He therefore speaks of "this apparent weakness" and "this area of confusion."

Dr. Walvoord does provide us with another meaning for the phrase "the Day of the Lord" when he wrote: "There seems to be some evidence that the Day of the Lord begins at once at the time of the translation of the church (cf. 1 Thess. 5:1-9). The same event which translates the church begins the Day of the Lord . . . . When the Day of grace ends with the translation of the church, the Day of the Lord begins at once" (p. 162 f.). So we must first accept the definition given concerning the Day of the Lord and go on from there to see whether the definition squares with the Scripture where the phrase is used. And it is here that the pretribulational position suffers from difficulties. What are they?

The first difficulty arises with the use of the term "the Day of the Lord" in 1 Thessalonians 5:2. Here it can surely be argued that the possibility for a pretribulation rapture is to be found in the text. One can say that the Day comes as a thief in the night in the sense that the rapture takes place before some of the known and predicted events of the tribulation period begin. Moreover Paul says that "God hath not appointed us to wrath," and if this is taken to mean deliverance from the terrors of the tribulation, it is appropriate. But the problem rises from Paul's second letter to the Thessalonians. In chapter one of that second letter, Paul is talking very specifically about the second advent of the Lord Jesus. He wrote:

> We ourselves glory in you in the churches of God for your patience and faith in all your persecutions and tribulations that ye endure. . . . And to you who are troubled rest with us, when the Lord Jesus shall be revealed from heaven with his mighty angels in flaming fire taking vengeance . . . when he shall come to be glorified in his saints and to be admired in all them that believe in that day [2 Thess. 1:4-10].

Paul is here writing to a specific church. He never once suggests that they will be raptured before Christ comes in flaming fire taking vengeance on them that know not God. Rather he quiets their fears in the midst of their troubles and says they are to be granted "rest with us" while they wait for the return of

Christ. There does not appear to be any pretribulational rapture in this Scripture. The problem grows in size when chapter two of Second Thessalonians is taken into account.

In verse one of chapter two Paul wrote:

> Now we beseech you, brethren, by the coming of our Lord Jesus Christ, and by our gathering unto him, that ye be not soon shaken in mind, or be troubled, neither by spirit, nor by word, nor by letter as from us, as that the day of Christ [in the Greek it is Lord] is at hand.

It takes little imagination to suppose that, accepting the definition of the phrase "the Day of the Lord" as suggested by Dr. Walvoord that Paul should have said to the Thessalonians immediately: "You can be sure that the Day of the Lord has not started because the Church has not been raptured. And before that Day starts you will be taken away." But he did nothing of the sort. He went on to do something which is still more troublesome to pretribulationism. He said that the Day of the Lord would not come until "there come a falling away first, and that man of sin be revealed, the son of perdition."

When this Scripture is taken literally, it can only mean that before the Day of the Lord comes, some known and predicted events must take place first. And he lists events that we know from other Scripture will take place during the tribulation period. This can only mean that the Church will go through the tribulation or at least some part of it. It is here that E. Schuyler English, in his book *Rethinking the Rapture*, comes to grips with the phrase *he apostasia* or *the apostasy*. He makes the claim that Liddell and Scott say there is another possible usage of the word *apostasia*, meaning *departure*. On that basis, he claims that the true meaning here is that the Day of the Lord will not take place until first there is the departure, that is the rapture of the Church. He takes this viewpoint for one simple reason. If the apostasy must take place first, then the Church will go through some part of the tribulation. Therefore he must rapture the Church before the apostasy takes place. This is circular reasoning for he uses the word *departure* for apostasy in order to prove what he has already assumed. In other words he *must* use *departure* for, if he does not, his case for a pretribulational rapture which he assumes is lost.

Is the use of the word *departure* for *apostasy* reasonable? In the first place, the church fathers to a man understood this chapter of second Thessalonians to be speaking about the apostasy. No version of the Bible uses the word *departure*. The King James uses the phrase *a falling away* which cannot mean *departure* unless it is used in the sense of departing from the faith, not the Church being caught up to meet the Lord in the air. The New International Version, which was put together by evangelical scholars, uses the phrase *the rebellion* which is far removed from *departure*. The Revised Standard Version uses the phrase *the rebellion*. If the word *apostasia* did refer to the rapture (departure), it would not follow logically what Paul said in verse one, "our gathering together unto him." It would seem to make Paul say, in effect, "Our gathering together unto him will not take place until the rapture (our gathering together unto him)," a nonsense statement.

Nowhere in the New Testament is *apostasia*, which appears only twice, translated *departure*. Thus it appears that the use of the word *departure* is forced on the text to protect the pre-tribulational rapture which is lost if the phrase *the apostasy* or *the rebellion* is used.

The phrase *the Day of the Lord* has been understood by pre-tribulational rapturists to be a period of time which begins with the rapture of the Church and goes on for the period of the tribulation or at least until the second advent of Jesus Christ. It is here that another grave problem arises from Paul's second chapter of Second Thessalonians. We will look at it first as though the phrase *the apostasy* means *the departure* and refers to the rapture of the Church before the Day of the Lord begins, rather than the apostasy of the churches.

Paul wrote that the Day of the Lord will not come *unless*, and quoting the Greek in the order the words appear, "unless comes the apostasy (or the departure) firstly and is revealed the man of lawlessness the son of perdition the (one) setting against and exalting himself over everything being called God or object of worship, so as him in the shrine of God to sit, showing himself that he is a god." Then Paul wrote about the mystery of lawlessness and the taking away of the restrainer. After this Jesus Christ shall consume the Wicked One with the spirit of his mouth and shall destroy him with the brightness of his coming. Thus the Day of the Lord will not and cannot come until the man of sin is made manifest and the mystery of lawlessness exhibited.

This rather clearly certifies that even if the Church were to be raptured before the tribulation, the Day of the Lord would still not begin until these other signs had been fulfilled. This forces us to ask the question whether the phrase the Day of the Lord does refer to the seven-year period known as the tribulation or whether it refers to a day at the end of the age when Christ comes to rapture the Church and to dispose of the Antichrist, the man of sin, the beast, and the false prophet. Any literal interpretation of Second Thessalonians leads to the conclusion that the Day of the Lord does not begin the period of the tribulation even if the Church were raptured before the tribulation because other events must occur before the Day of the Lord commences.

THE FIRST RESURRECTION

A second and troublesome problem for the pretribulational position is the phrase the first resurrection. On the surface it would appear that the phrase points to a single event that occurs and then does not occur again. The pretribulational position requires that this phrase be understood to mean that there are several resurrections occurring at different times within the term the first resurrection. Are there any grounds for supposing this to be so?

The saints of God will be raised from the dead at the time of the rapture. This is stated clearly in First Thessalonians four. That Scripture says: "For the Lord himself shall descend from heaven with a shout, with the voice of the archangel, and with the trump of God: and the dead in Christ shall rise first." The rising of the dead in Christ is a resurrection. Of that there can be no doubt. Dr. Scofield, in his footnote for this Scripture wrote as follows:

> Not church saints only, but all bodies of the saved, of whatever dispensation, are included in the first resurrection (see 1 Cor. 15:52, note), as here described, but it is

peculiarly the "blessed hope" of the Church (cf. Mt. 24:42; 25:13; Lk. 12:36-48; Acts 1:11; Phil. 3:20, 21; Tit. 2:11-13).

Several peculiarities should be noted before we discuss the term *the first resurrection* as used by Dr. Scofield. He refers to verses in Matthew and Luke about the blessed hope of the Church which he says is the rapture. But the verses in Matthew and Luke which speak of the coming of the Lord ("Watch therefore: for ye know not what hour your Lord doth come" [Matt. 24:42]; "Watch therefore, for ye know neither the day nor the hour wherein the Son of man cometh" [Matt. 25:13]; "Be ye therefore ready also: for the Son of man cometh at an hour when ye think not" [Luke 12:40]), never mention the Church which, according to Dr. Scofield, is a mystery unfolded *after* Pentecost and explicated in the epistles.

How these passages from Matthew and Luke can be understood to be the *blessed hope of the Church* is indeed a mystery. Moreover, these verses say nothing about the time when this will happen, so that even if they did refer to the rapture or the blessed hope which is the rapture, there is nothing in these verses to determine whether it will be a pretribulational rapture. In fact, in Matthew 24 the word to watch is preceded by a terrible description of tribulation which comes before the statement about the coming of the Lord. But the greater problem still exists about the first resurrection to which we now turn our attention.

All who hold to a pretribulational rapture must also hold to the notion that the first resurrection includes more than one resurrection event separated by a period of time of not less than seven years. They say there are really two first resurrections; one at the time of the rapture when the saints who are dead are raised from the dead, and another at the end of the age when Jesus has beaten back the Devil in the battle of Armageddon. Again we look at one of Dr. Scofield's notes:

Two resurrections are yet future, which are inclusive of "all that are in the graves" (John 5:28). These are distinguished as "of life" (1 Cor. 15:22, 23; 1 Thess. 4:14-17; Rev. 20:4), and "of judgment" (John 5:28, 29; Rev. 20:11-13). They are separated by a period of one thousand years [Rev. 20:5]. The "first resurrection" that "unto life," will occur at the second coming of Christ (1 Cor. 15:23), the saints of the O.T. and church ages meeting Him in the air (1 Thess. 4:16, 17); while the martyrs of the tribulation, who also have part in the first resurrection (Rev. 20:4), are raised at the end of the great tribulation [p. 1228].

The rapture passage in First Thessalonians says nothing whatever about the first resurrection. It simply speaks of a resurrection of the dead at the time of the rapture. Only in Revelation is there found the statement: "This is the first resurrection" (Rev. 20:5). When the context is examined it will become plain immediately that it is spoken of in connection with

them that were beheaded for the witness of Jesus, and for the word of God, and which had not worshipped the beast, neither had received his mark upon their foreheads, or in their hands; and they lived and reigned with Christ a thousand years [Rev. 20:4, 5].

This certainly seems to be speaking primarily about those who were beheaded or martyred during the great tribulation period. They were brought to life and lived and reigned with Christ for a thousand years. There has been no such resurrection to date. When it occurs, it indicates that the people spoken of will be on earth with Christ which can only mean the millennium. No direct word appears either about those who still were alive when this happened as is true in First Thessalonians chapter four, nor does it specifically mention the dead in Christ from earlier ages. But it does say that this is the first resurrection. It does *not* say it is the second phase of the first resurrection, allowing for an earlier resurrection in a pretribulational sense. It constitutes a problem for both the pretribulational and posttribulational positions. Since Second Thessalonians chapter two does speak of the Day of the Lord coming *after* the man of sin has been revealed and so on, one can *infer* that the saints of all ages will be involved in this first resurrection spoken of in the Revelation.

Scofield, in his note on First Thessalonians chapter four, includes *all* the Old Testament dead in the rapture, that is Israel and the Church. If Revelation chapter twenty is to be taken very literally, it is hard to see how the Old Testament saints could be included in this first resurrection. Perhaps this is why some pretribulationists have altered the new Scofield Bible to take out the statement that the Old Testament saints who are not in the Church are raptured at the same time the Church is raptured and those dead Old Testament believers are resurrected. If the Old Testament saints are not raised at the rapture from the pretribulational viewpoint, when are they raised to life? Surely not from Revelation chapter twenty, which seems to be speaking about the tribulation saints. No other place in Scripture speaks about the resurrection of the Old Testament saints apart from these two passages as the event relates to timing. They seem to be left in limbo.

If the Old Testament saints are raptured along with the Church in a pretribulational rapture, is not the dispensational distinction between Israel and the Church lost? And once that distinction is impaired, a posttribulational rapture becomes far more likely. If Israel of the Old Testament is left to be raised from the dead in the event spoken of in the Revelation, the passage does not say so explicitly and we are back again to two resurrections in any event: that of the Church earlier and of the great tribulational dead later so that the term *the first resurrection* loses force and effect. It appears to me that pretribulationists and posttribulationists must read something into the text in Revelation chapter twenty in order to make their respective positions square with their exegesis.

Most pretribulationists seem to say that the Church will not reign with Christ on earth during the millennium. Israel will be on earth during this period and the Church will be in heaven. This creates a tough problem when considered in the light of the ubiquity of Jesus Christ. By ubiquity we mean that Christ is in a body and wherever Christ is, his body must be also. By reason of the incarnation and the *kenosis* in which Jesus emptied himself, the Church has always understood that wherever Jesus is really present, his body must be present also.

This distinction lies at the heart of the ordinance or sacrament of the Lord's Table. If Christ is *really* present at the sacrament of the supper, then he must be there in his body. So the Roman Catholic Church teaches the real presence of Christ in the Mass. That is precisely why people in the Baptist tradition say that Christ is only symbolically present in the elements at the Lord's Table. He is not really present. The God-man is in a body. Wherever the God-man is, the body must be also.

How, then, can Christ be in heaven with the Church and on earth with Israel all at the same time? Is it not far more likely that the Church and Israel will both be on earth during the millennium? And is it not likely that Israel is numbered among the saints in the Church? Does not this question demand a re-examination of the viewpoint that there are two peoples of God: Israel and the Church which are separate entities that cannot be fused, intermingled, or be considered as one body in Christ.

THE WRATH TO COME

The period of the great tribulation is divided in Scripture into two parts of three and a half years each. During the first half of the tribulation, the wrath of man is poured out. The beast out of the sea and the beast out of the earth will have come forth. They will collaborate with each other in their persecutions. The Book of the Revelation (13:11 ff.) describes how men will be given the mark of the beast, the number being 666. Whoever refuses to bear the mark will be martyred. Will the wrath of man keep people from being saved? Not at all!

John in chapter seven makes clear that there will be Jews and Gentiles saved during this period. 144,000 Jews from among the tribes of Israel will be saved. The angel said: "Hurt not the earth, neither the sea, nor the trees, till we have sealed the servants of our God in their foreheads" (7:3). We must remember that the total number of Jews in the whole world does not exceed four-tenths of one percent of the world's population. The number of Israelites sealed is, of course, far smaller than this. Numerically the Jews are so few as to be negligible. Their importance in God's plan, then, is astronomically greater than their numbers. On the other hand John says of the Gentiles:

> After this I beheld, and lo, a great multitude, which no man could number, of all nations, and kindreds, and people, and tongues, stood before the throne, and before the Lamb, clothed with white robes, and palms in their hands.... These are they which came out of the great

tribulation, and have washed their robes, and made them white in the blood of the Lamb [7:9, 14].

It is evident that the multitude of Gentiles who are saved during the first half of the tribulation are spoken of as being virtually innumerable, which simply means here a very large number. Apparently they refused to bear the mark of the beast. And they have come to know Christ as their Savior. Are these Gentiles to be numbered as among the Israelites? Nothing in Scripture warrants such a designation. Are they to be numbered among those who are members of the body of Christ the Church? If the Church has been raptured before the tribulation and that is the end of the Church so that none can be added to it, then there must be a third group of people besides Israel and the Church. But Scripture allows for no such possibility. They must be part of the Church of Jesus Christ. Thus, even if the Church as known by God before the beginning of the tribulation has been raptured, there are still people who will be saved and who are members of the Church who will go through the tribulation. Thus, some part of the Church must go through the tribulation if this be true. This makes for a real problem for the pretribulationist.

On the other hand, posttribulationism has its own problem at this point. If the Church does go through the tribulation and if these multitudes who are saved during this period are members of the Church, what about the Scripture which asserts that "God hath not appointed us to wrath, but to obtain salvation by our Lord Jesus Christ" (1 Thess. 5:9). The Greek word used for wrath here is the same word used in Romans 2:5, in Matthew 3:7, and Luke 3:7 which all speak of the wrath of God. The word also appears in the Revelation having to do with the second half of the tribulation period when the wrath of God is poured out on this earth. Only two possibilities exist: either the Church has been raptured before the wrath of God is poured out, but it would most likely be a midtribulation rapture coming after the Church has experienced the persecution of the Antichrist; or God would supernaturally preserve his people from his wrath even as he protected the children of Israel from the plagues which wrought havoc among the Egyptians. Thus the phrase "not appointed us to wrath" as used in First Thessalonians 5:12 probably means what it does in Matthew 3:7 and

Luke 3:7 where it does not refer to the Church at all but to the final judgment and the lake of fire.

In Revelation 16:1, where the Scripture reads "the seven bowls of the wrath of God," the word used for wrath is a different word meaning the *anger* of God. The seven bowls of wrath are the anger or wrath of God and this aspect of the tribulation comes during the last half of the seven-year period. It is hardly possible to suppose that the multitudes coming out of the great tribulation who have washed their robes and made them white in the blood of the Lamb would have been martyred by the outpouring of the wrath of God. God does not make martyrs by pouring out his wrath on his own people. Martyrs are made by the enemies of God. We know from Scripture that not all of God's people are martyred by the Antichrist by the end of the first half of the tribulation period.

In Revelation 16:15, Jesus is speaking. He says: "Blessed is he who is awake, keeping his garments that he may not go naked and be seen exposed." Obviously these must be saints of God who do not have the mark of the beast on them and who have not been martyred. Shortly the battle of Armageddon is to be fought. These saints have not experienced the wrath of God. In addition Jesus Christ says, "Lo, I am coming like a thief." This is strange language if the Church has been raptured, for elsewhere in the Gospels and the Epistles where the idea of imminence or soon coming of the Lord for the Church is mentioned, the phrase "like a thief in the night" is used.

Pretribulationists understand this phrase to mean both imminence and unexpectedness. Yet Christ uses it here when the time with respect to the second advent can be fixed with virtually absolute certainty. For pretribulationists, the second advent occurs seven years after the rapture of the Church when the "Day of the Lord" begins, which is the seventieth week of Daniel. Once the tribulation begins, seven years must elapse before the end of the age. Thus the phrase "like a thief," contrary to pretribulational understanding, should not be understood to mean imminence in "an any-moment sense," but only that when the time comes Jesus will come like a thief even if it is only a twenty-four hour period. Within that short period, he could come when we were not ready for him unless we were to stay awake and watch.

REVELATION CHAPTER FOUR AND THE RAPTURE

Pretribulationists generally are agreed that the Church is raptured at the beginning of chapter four of the Revelation. Chapter three outlines the messages to the seven churches, each one of which is mentioned specifically. Other churches were in existence at this time so that it cannot be said that the seven churches were the only known churches and thus comprised the whole body of Christ, the Church. Unless it can be established that the messages to the seven churches were in fact messages to all of the churches, then it would not follow that the call "Come up hither" (Rev. 4:1) applied to the entire Church. At best it would apply only to the seven churches if the calls are understood to have something to do with the rapture.

The language of Revelation 4:1, 2 is such that a pretribulation rapture must be read into the verses, for it is by no means clear that the verses speak of the rapture explicitly. The Scripture says "after this I looked" which has to do with John. "The first voice which I heard" also has to do with John. The command, "Come up hither, and I will shew thee things to come" has a singular "thee," not the plural. And "immediately I was in the spirit" speaks only of John and says nothing whatever of the seven churches. As John proceeds, he says, "I was in the spirit" (v. 2); "I saw four and twenty elders" (v. 4); "I saw in the right hand of him" (5:1); "I wept much" (5:4); "I beheld" (5:6); "I beheld" (5:11); "Heard I saying" (5:13); and this personal witness continues.

C. I. Scofield is not at all dogmatic that chapter four begins with the rapture of the Church. He wrote: "This call *seems* [my italics] clearly to indicate the fulfillment of 1 Thessalonians 4:14-17. The word "church" does not again occur in the Revelation till all is fulfilled." He uses the word *seems* indicating his own uncertainty. He speaks of it as being the fulfillment of 1 Thessalonians four. Any examination of the passage shows that it does not deal with the *time* of the rapture. Nor does he refer to 2 Thessalonians two to prove the pretribulational rapture of the Church either in this footnote in the Revelation (p. 1334) or in the footnote to Second Thessalonians two. Revelation 4:1, 2 is unclear, and to use it to support either the pretribulational or the posttribulational position is out of place.

THE MARRIAGE SUPPER OF THE LAMB

In Revelation 19:7 ff., the marriage supper of the Lamb is described. Apparently it takes place just before the second advent of Jesus Christ as King of Kings and Lord of Lords. Who is the wife or the bride to which reference is made? C. I. Scofield has a curious note about this:

> The "Lamb's wife" here is the "bride" (Rev. 21:9), the Church, identified with the "heavenly Jerusalem" (Heb. 12:22, 23), and to be distinguished from Israel, the adulterous and repudiated "wife" of Jehovah, yet to be restored (Isa. 54:1-10; Hos. 2:1-17), who is identified with the earth (Hos. 2:23). A forgiven and restored *wife* could not be called either a *virgin* (2 Cor. 11:2, 3), or a *bride*.

First, we know that Israel at this point is back in the land and is under assault by her foes. The Lord will come to rescue his people Israel. Whoever among those of Israel who are at that time among the redeemed obviously are not included in the marriage supper of the Lamb if it is for the Church and if Israel and the Church are separate. The participants in the marriage supper are called saints (Rev. 19:8). The word *church*, however, nowhere appears in this passage. Dr. Scofield does what some pretribulationists will not do. He says the wife or bride is the Church. If that is true, then the Church appears earlier than in Revelation 22:16 even though the word Church is not used. If the wife or bride is the Church and the Church is raptured before the tribulation begins, then the marriage supper is delayed by approximately seven years. Why should there be a gap? Would it not be consistent to suppose that it is at this point that the Church is raptured and its members invited to the marriage supper? Since the word *saints* is used for the members of the Church consistently in the epistles, why should it not here be understood to be the Church which has just been raptured? If this is true it leaves some problems for which there is no easy answer.

At the coming of the Lord, Israel is mentioned prominently

in Zechariah, for example. In the Old Testament prophetic writings prominence is given to Israel, its being regathered in the land, the rebuilding of the temple, and a period of peace and plenty. It is hardly to be supposed that, as amillennialists say, the Church is the new Israel and that all of the prophecies pertaining to Israel are fulfilled in the Church. Israel, in the land today and in control of the city of Jerusalem, has nothing whatever to do with the Church, for the Israelites are back in the land in unbelief. They are not now members of the body of Christ. There are a number of prophecies made about Israel which have not yet been fulfilled. Ezekiel specifies that there will be the rebuilding of the temple and he describes the details so precisely that to nullify his prophetic word would do violence to Scripture and to fulfilled prophecy. It is incredible to suppose that God the Holy Spirit went to all that trouble to describe that which will never become a reality. Whether all of these prophecies will be fulfilled before the second advent or whether some of them will take place during the millennium remains to be determined.

The Apostle Paul in Romans 9—11 interrupts his discourse after the eighth chapter to focus on Israel. He indicates that God still has a concern for his people Israel. And there is a time coming when all Israel will be saved. It is difficult to fit Israel fully into the picture with the Church and commingle them so as to impair any distinction between them. Here the pretribulationist and the dispensationalist have a point which should not be overlooked. Neither dispensationalism nor reformed theology, which calls the Church the new Israel, can produce a foolproof case for the respective viewpoints. Both sides are left with problems.

We may be forced to conclude that the reconciliation of the data for both Israel and the Church may rest in the secret will of God and has not been fully revealed to us and will not be revealed to us until the events of the future unfold before our eyes. It is, of course, far easier to be a confirmed dispensationalist or a confirmed Reformed theologian while pushing the problem areas to one side. It might be better for us to forget our systems and acknowledge that we do not yet see clearly with respect to the conflicting evidences. This does not mean we should cease our efforts to fit the pieces of the puzzle together.

What we need today, in the light of the many changes which have taken place in the last several decades, is a prophetic conference for those who are thoroughly in accord with the view that the Bible itself is utterly trustworthy. The crucial issues could be discussed openly and the varying viewpoints not only presented but replied to and argued. It is highly unlikely that the proponents of either viewpoint will surrender their position but at least it may result in further refinements of both positions, taking into account the developments of a prophetic nature which have taken place in the last two decades. Such a conference would be a healthy corrective to isolated conferences in which only one position is promoted. It would also acquaint the people in the pews with the data for the differing positions and give them food for thought.

A number of pretribulationists hold that view because they do not want to go through the tribulation. Their attitude derives more from that desire than from a serious interaction with the data. If the Church does go through the tribulation, some who hold the view may be badly shaken because they have assumed their view is so certain that any loss of it may have serious consequences. A prophetic conference could make them aware of the fact that neither viewpoint claims explicit support from Scripture. The reason why it is important for pretribulationists to understand this is that they have everything to lose if they are wrong, whereas the posttribulationists have nothing to lose.

If it should turn out that the pretribulationists are correct, the posttribulationists will learn of their error when they are caught up before the tribulation. But having been raptured, they have nothing to lose and everything to gain. Their *disappointment* will turn to joy because they will be in the presence of Christ. Their faith will not be threatened, and they will not be shaken in the possession of their faith on this score. It is therefore more important for the pretribulationists to learn that neither view is certain than for posttribulationists to do so.

It is also important for pretribulationists to learn that those who entertain this view are quite divided among themselves.

Thus Dr. Walvoord can fault the early advocates of this view. And the Scofield Bible has been altered at important points in the new Scofield Bible. And the Scofield Bible itself is inconsistent in its presentation of the position. When these facts are known, it will make all holders of the viewpoint more tentative and less dogmatic. This will be a considerable gain.

EVANGELIZATION DURING THE TRIBULATION

There is another vexing problem which the holders of the pretribulational viewpoint must wrestle with seriously. I have not personally seen the argument I have in mind presented in any of the writings I have examined to this point. The question I will ask staggers my imagination and appears difficult to answer. In adducing it, a scenario must be laid down first.

We will suppose, for the purpose of our discussion, that the Church will be raptured before the tribulation period begins, or as the Day of the Lord commences. We will suppose that Jesus came for the Church today—the very day the reader is perusing this book. What would the implications of that coming be?

First, it would mean that no further prophecies remained to be fulfilled in advance of that coming. Moreover, *all* unfulfilled prophecies would then have to be fulfilled following the rapture and in a period of seven years. For those who think a period of time may elapse between the rapture of the Church and the seventieth week of Daniel, we can only say that this is pure invention. It has no support in Scripture. Once this door is opened, the period of time could be a thousand years with the Holy Spirit withdrawn and no church witness during that period. So we will stay with the traditional view that the catching away of the Church is followed by the seventieth week.

During the seven-year period, certain events must occur. The Roman Empire must be reestablished. The temple must be rebuilt and the sacrifices recommenced. The Israelis must enter into a covenant with the Antichrist, who is yet unknown. In order that a covenant be made with him, he must quickly come to the forefront. During this short period, the Israelis will evangelize the world, something the Church has not done in two thousand years, and this will take place with the Holy Spirit having been withdrawn. The Antichrist will place the mark of the beast on earth's multitudes and millions upon millions of believers will be martyred. In the middle of the period, the covenant between the Antichrist and the Israelis will be broken and then the wrath of God will be poured out.

Multiplied millions of troops must be assembled in the Near East to fight the last battle of Armageddon. Time and space limitations must be taken into account, and we know that simply keeping such large armies supplied and serviced will be a massive operation requiring a considerable space of time just to make preparations for it. Food, armaments, oil, and other supplies for the number of soldiers said to be involved in this conflict is mind-boggling. For every soldier there must be four or five support and supply people behind him. If they move on foot, it would take much time. If they have modern vehicles of transportation, there is nowhere enough to care for such armies now and there wouldn't be for some time to come.

What caps the climax to this scenario is that fact that when the rapture of the Church takes place, every last Christian will be caught away immediately. This means there will not be a single evangelist, a single missionary anywhere in the world of more than four billion people. There will be no Christian schools, no Christian radio and television programs. The Antichrist will not be able to find a single Christian to persecute nor anyone who is a Christian on whom to print the mark of the beast or to kill if he refuses to receive the mark. The Scripture asks "And how shall they hear without a preacher? And how shall they preach, except they be sent?" (Rom. 10:14, 15). At this time, there is no one to be sent and there is no one to send anybody. There are no missionary agencies, no recruits, nothing. Since there are no preachers, how will people get converted? There will be no converted Israelis sitting by to take up the slack. Every converted Israeli in this age is a member of the body of Christ the Church so all of them will have been caught away, too.

Thus, in the ensuing seventieth week, vast, undreamed of multitudes must become Christians. There will be no mature believers around to nurture them or help them. They will have little knowledge of the intricacies of Christian doctrine and especially eschatology. The 144,000 Jews who come to the New Testament in salvation will be no better off than their Gentile friends. Moreover, world evangelization is to take place among the peoples of the world who speak in thousands of different tongues. Reaching them in their own languages in seven years is no small job! The matter is further complicated by reason of the fact that John in his Revelation states that only those who do not have the mark of the beast are among the elect. But with all the Christians caught away, vast multitudes of people will undoubtedly have received the mark of the beast before they heard the good news of salvation. Already having been marked, there is no provision in Scripture for repudiating that mark and they probably will have already worshiped the beast during the time they were unconverted.

The problems may be fewer in comparison for the midtribulational rapturists, but it is equally difficult to perceive how they, in three and a half years, with every last Christian gone, can do what will still need to be done according to the prophetic Word. From that perspective, every Jew and every Gentile saved during the first half of the tribulation must of necessity be a member of the Church of Jesus Christ and will therefore be caught away in the rapture. Once more we will face a world without a single Christian witness with multiplied millions still to be saved and to be martyred when they refuse to bear the mark of the beast.

These are matters which require the most thoughtful consideration and demand adequate answers if pretribulationism is to remain an option in eschatology.

I personally would like very much to hold to pretribulationism with dogmatic certainty. But the data, in my opinion, seems to lean more in the direction of the posttribulation position. However, posttribulationism leaves me without satisfactory answers about Israel in relation to the end times, the Church, and the lack of explicit biblical details which would answer my unanswered questions. Of one thing I am absolutely certain. There is a rapture. And I must let God be God. He holds the pieces of the puzzle in his hands and whatever he wants to do will be perfect when I understand how the pieces fit together. I am ready for either a pretribulational or a posttribulational rapture. But there is one question which remains to be discussed: believing that the signs of the times point to the soon coming of our Lord, how then shall we live while we wait with expectancy for that for which the people of God have looked for two thousand years?

8

HOW THEN SHOULD WE LIVE?

IN THE LIGHT OF WHAT HAS BEEN SAID IN THE PRE-
ceding chapters of this book we must ask the question: If we
are already in the closing days of this age or will be shortly,
how then shall we live? Stated another way we might ask: If
the Lord's coming is delayed, should we live differently from
how we would live if we knew for certain that he will come in
your lifetime and mine?

The question, How then should we live? is vital because
many people make important decisions on the basis of their
assumption that the Lord is coming shortly. Some young people do not bother to complete their education, for they think the
time is short and want to evangelize to a finish before the Lord
comes. The sister of a dear friend of mine thought her brother
should not waste his time going to college and medical school
in preparation for the mission field for the Lord was coming
very soon. He did it anyway. When he finally returned from
China he began a long and honored career in medicine and
Christian work and has rendered yeoman service to Christ and
the Church through scores of activities which have been ex-
ceedingly fruitful. His sister died a few years ago, over seventy
years of age, still believing that the Lord was coming shortly.
If her brother had followed her counsel he would have led a
different sort of life and would have contributed far less to the
work of Christ's kingdom.

I have heard Christian husbands say they would not buy life
insurance policies to protect their families because the Lord
was coming soon and insurance would do them no good. Some
of these men died, leaving their wives and children to suffer
hardships from their lack of foresight. Others have said that
buying life insurance demonstrates a lack of faith in God to
provide. So they refuse to purchase this form of economic pro-
tection for their families, whether they think the coming of
the Lord is upon them or not. How should we respond to such

attitudes? What does the Bible have to say to us?

Several principles come to mind as we think about the question: How then shall we live? The first principle is: We should always assume that the coming of the Lord may be delayed for a thousand years. I am personally convinced that we have come close to the consummation of the age. But when making decisions, I must choose as though I may be wrong. Thus, for example, I must provide for my wife as best I can subsequent to my death. The second principle is that the coming of the Lord may occur during my lifetime but that possibility should not cause me to change prudential decisions based on the first premise that the Lord's coming may be delayed for a thousand years. The reason for this approach is easy enough for all of us to understand. There is one sense in which the Lord will come for me during my lifetime. He will come for me at death if he does not come for me by the rapture and his second advent. The seventeen-year-old girl or boy does not know, if the Lord tarries, whether he or she has a year, a decade, or seventy more years before death strikes.

If I were seventeen and knew for certain I had only three years to live, I suspect I would forego entering college since I would never finish. But this knowledge of the time of my death lies in the secret will of God, not the revealed will of God. Therefore I should act as though I were to live to be eighty. So I follow that assumption and proceed with my college education if it is in the will of God. If death comes, so be it.

Friends of mine have had children who died while still in college. They died in the will of God and that is all that really counts. In general, then, we should make decisions based on the possibility that the coming of the Lord will be delayed and that each of us might live to be eighty, more or less.

A third principle is to take into account the nature of the times. From the historical perspective, the times have differed widely century after century. There may be times when the state of affairs are such that marriage should be eschewed, or higher education abandoned. The Apostle Paul said: "Brethren, the time is short: it remaineth, that both they that have wives be as though they had none . . . He that is unmarried careth for the things that belong to the Lord, how he may please the Lord . . . . So then he that giveth her in marriage doeth well;

but he that giveth her not in marriage doeth better" (1 Cor. 7:29 ff.). Paul neither forbade marriage nor encouraged it per se. But he did think the times were such that perhaps Christians would do better by remaining single. However, he counseled them to marry rather than to remain single if they could not contain themselves.

THE LORDSHIP OF CHRIST

With these few principles in mind we can proceed with concrete recommendations about how Christians ought to live. We know from Scripture that all Christians should let Jesus be Lord of their lives. The Bible teaches that Jesus is Savior and Lord. He can be Savior without being Lord in an experiential manner. Theologically we must affirm that Jesus is Lord whether he becomes this in experience or not. But all Christians should experience the Lordship of Christ. We mean by this that they are to be under his control and are to do his will for their lives. Many Christians cannot say that Jesus is Lord in this sense. He has saved them, but they go their own ways and do what they wish to do without seeking what he wants. Irrespective of times and seasons, Jesus must become Lord of our lives if we are to live as we ought.

THE FULLNESS OF THE SPIRIT

Every Christian should be filled with the Holy Spirit. We know from Scripture that not every believer is filled with the Holy Spirit. We learn this from Acts chapter six when the apostles set up the requirements for the office of deacon. The Scripture says: "Look ye out from among you seven men of honest report, full of the Holy Spirit and wisdom" (Acts 6:3). If all the men were filled with the Holy Spirit this injunction would never have been laid down. Similarly not all men were or ever will be given the gift of wisdom. Only those who had it were to be considered for the office of deacon. In Ephesians 5:18 Paul wrote: "Be not drunk with wine, wherein is excess; but be filled with the Spirit." Again, if all believers were filled with the Holy Spirit this statement would not make sense. But not all were filled with the Holy Spirit. So Paul commanded all

believers to be filled. Moreover, he would not have commanded this if it were not possible for all of them to be filled. Thus
no one can be excused from being filled with the Spirit on the
strength of the notion that this is something available only to
some but not for all of God's people.

Whatever the day or the age, being filled with the Spirit is
a vital necessity for a dynamic and effective Christian walk
and witness. The mark of being filled with the Spirit is the
living of a holy life. It also will result in the presence of the
fruit of the Spirit in that life. In Galatians 5:22-25, Paul spoke
about the quality of this sort of life:

> But the fruit of the Spirit is love, joy, peace, longsuffering,
> gentleness, goodness, faith, meekness, temperance:
> against such there is no law. And they that are Christ's
> have crucified the flesh with the affections and lusts. If
> we live in the Spirit, let us also walk in the Spirit.

The Scripture spells out the method and means whereby
we may be filled with the Spirit: (1) Jesus Christ must become
Lord of our lives; (2) we must confess whatever sins we know
of in our lives and be forgiven; (3) we must ask God to fill us
with his Holy Spirit; (4) we accept and receive the filling of
the Holy Spirit by faith and go out to act as though we have
been so filled.

THINKING CHRISTIANLY

Every Christian should think Christianly. There are few Christians who think this way. Our world has been largely secularized as a result of the Renaissance and the Enlightenment.
Thus, the Christian mind has become a rare commodity. In
many instances it no longer exists. When an unbeliever becomes a Christian, regeneration does something positive to his
mind. It makes it possible for him to think as a Christian, but
it does not guarantee that he will think this way—only that he
may do so.

To think Christianly is to think the way Christ thinks. It is
not to conform the mind to the mold of the world but to let
Christ become the model for the thought life. The Christian
mind, then, is to be metamorphosed or renewed or lifted up to

a higher plane so that it operates in agreement with the mind of Christ. We are to think his thoughts after him. Proper thought will lead to proper action or conduct.

The revealed will of God becomes the touchstone of conduct. The law of God becomes embedded in our characters so that we follow it almost unconsciously. No effort is made to justify fornication, adultery, homosexual conduct, envy, pride, lying, stealing, cheating, and covetousness. From God's perspective, these sins are looked upon as being characteristic of the old man, not the new man who has been renewed unto holiness by the power of the Spirit of God.

When believers think Christianly, they seek and obtain the knowledge of God's will for their lives. Every vocation that is not forbidden becomes holy to God when his children do the divine will. Every calling is sacred, not profane, although the work may not be thought of as sacred because it does not relate directly to the Christian ministry. This is not so. The factory worker, the lawyer, the truck driver, and storekeeper may be thought of as engaging in secular vocations. But if they are Christians, these vocations are just as sacred as the ministry, the mission field, or teaching in a Christian school. Whatever is in the will of God is sacred, not profane. We can wash dishes to the glory of God just as much as we can preach sermons to his glory. Every believer should know that what he or she is doing is the will of God for his or her life and is a sacred calling in which he or she is to glorify God.

THE CHURCH

Every Christian should become a member of a visible church that is sound in the faith; a church where the gospel is preached in its fullness, where evangelism and missions are given primacy, and where Christian action in all spheres of life is taught. Church membership is not optional. It is the will of God for everyone who is regenerated. Attendance at the services of the church should be regular. We are not to neglect the assembling of ourselves together as evidently some Christians did in the New Testament (Heb. 10:25). Worship is an essential part of the Christian life. While we can worship by ourselves at home, the Scripture demands public worship in an assembly of gathered people of God who make use of the ordinances or sacraments of the Lord's Supper and baptism.

This admonition is especially relevant in our generation where the electronic media have caused multitudes of Christians to forsake worship in local churches while they stay at home to participate in religious services over radio or television. This works havoc in the lives of those who do so. Such people disobey the express commandment of God. No one who stays at home can obey the commandment to gather together with other believers for the worship of God. And the ordinances or sacraments cannot be celebrated by an individual alone. Christians manage to get to work when the weather is bad or they are feeling tired. They should be more diligent in gathering together in a house of worship regardless of the weather or their feelings.

TITHING

God has commanded His people to tithe. The often-used excuse that we are under grace, not under law, is not consistent with thinking Christianly. Certainly under grace we believers can do no less than the Israelites did under law. The presumption that being under grace somehow delivers us from the commandments of God is unsound on the face of it. The commandment that we shall love God with "all thy heart, and with all thy soul, and with all thy mind" is unbreakable. Once we admit there is one commandment which is forever true, the door is opened wide to other commandments which continue forever in time. Just as it is always wrong to commit adultery, so it is always wrong for me to withhold from God that which belongs to him.

David said, "All things come from thee O Lord and of thine own have we given thee" (1 Chron. 29:14). Since everything I have has been given to me by God, I have an obligation to recognize his bounty by returning to him for the use of his church a portion of what he has given to me. The tithe is God's portion and symbolizes the hard fact that all I have belongs to God in the first place. The tithe symbolizes the Lordship of

Christ over my life and is a concrete testimony to that relation-ship.

In fact, the New Testament Scripture lays down basic prin-ciples to guide us in our giving. We are to do it regularly upon the first day of the week (1 Cor. 16:2). And we are to give as God has prospered us. Thus it is to be proportionate. The more we have, the more we should give proportionately.

The local church of which we are members should be first on our list with respect to giving. Some say that the entire tithe should be given to the local church. Surely if a believer has the desire to give money to enterprises not directly connected with the local church, he or she can give through the local church by designating that the church send it to those enter-prises on behalf of the one who gives the money.

Christians who do not have immediate relatives such as children and grandchildren should give serious thought to leaving their estates to their churches or enterprises of a Chris-tian sort which they approve of. Even those who have children and grandchildren should ask themselves what portion of their estates should go to Christian work at their deaths. The com-mand of the proverbist holds true today: "Honor the Lord with thy substance, and with the firstfruits of all thine increase" (Prov. 3:9). And God has promised there and elsewhere that those who follow his instructions with reference to money he will bless and prosper whether it be materially or spiritually (Prov. 3:10; Mal. 3:10, 11).

DEVOTIONAL LIFE

The cultivation of the devotional life is stressed everywhere in Scripture and very particularly in the life of our Lord. Jesus knew the Word of God and he prayed often and long. When we read and study the Scripture, God speaks to us; when we pray, we speak to God. This two-way street must be traversed daily and the way kept open at all times.

The devotional use of the Bible is important. The daily use of it and the systematic application of it to life produces holy living and fruitful service. I make it a habit to read five pages of the Bible every day. Sometimes I read more than that. I begin with the book of Genesis, then Matthew, then back to the Old Testament and Exodus. Then comes the Gospel of Mark and so on. Using this systematic approach, I read through the Bible by the middle of December each year. I have done this for forty years. I also use the Bible for sermon preparation, for books I write and for study Bibles I have put together. The Bible is the one book in my library which I have read more than any other book. This is the way it should be. At the table we use daily Bible readings and other devotional material according to time and situation.

Not all of the Bible is of equal usefulness to us in the Christian life and walk. But all of the Bible is important and forms a complete package. Even those parts which, on the surface, seem the least significant, are worthy of our attention because they form part of the whole revelation of God. They often yield treasures we never anticipated but which the Holy Spirit who is our Teacher brings to our attention. It is the Spirit who makes the Bible real to us and seals it to our hearts' use. Thus we should read it under the Lordship of Christ and in the fullness of the Holy Spirit's power in our lives.

We should read devotional classics which have blessed the Church through the ages. I can attest to the fact that at a certain point of time in my own life the Holy Spirit used Oswald Chamber's little classic, *My Utmost for His Highest* to bring me to the place where I gladly made Jesus the Lord of my life and committed my life to him for whatever he wished me to be and do. That was the most important spiritual decision I made after I had been born into the kingdom of God through faith in Christ.

Christians should study the Bible too. They can do this by the use of commentaries, biographical study, and subject and theme studies covering all the places in Scripture where they are used, and by continually reviewing the great doctrines of the Christian faith. Eschatology, or the study of the last things, is one of the important theological themes we ought to study so that we can recognize the signs of the times and encourage our hearts in the certainty of Christ's second coming even as we wait for it with patience.

Bible memorization should play a role in our use of God's

Word. We are to hide the Word of God in our hearts. There are people who love Christ and who have been deprived of Bibles. They can only use what they have memorized. Given the nature of our times, the day may come when we in the western world may find that the Word of God has been taken away from us physically and we are left with only that which we can recall to mind. We may have to copy down what we remember, not only for our own use but also for the edification of the saints of God who may remember fewer verses of Scripture than we do. There are places where people do not have access to the Word of God. Bibles are not to be found in any of the Gulag Archipelagos. And despite the often repeated story that there are plenty of Bibles circulating in the Soviet Union, this is simply not the case. Nor are Bibles often available to the people of Red China.

Satan has for his major target the two Words of God: he wars against the Word of God incarnate, even Jesus Christ the Righteous One, and the Word of God written, the Bible. The fewer Bibles there are around the more gleeful Satan becomes. Even when the Bible is available, Satan snatches it from the good ground on which it might fall so that it does not bring forth fruit. And since we cannot use what we do not know or remember, the less we have of the Bible the more successful Satan is in his cosmic warfare against the Lord Jesus. However, a Bible which is available to us is of no use unless we read it and apply it to our lives. Some Christians have blank pages in their Bibles. By this I mean pages they've never read, or if they have read these pages they do not apply them to their everyday lives.

The Bible must be applied after we have read it. The Jews of Jesus' day knew the Bible but they applied it wrongly. Satan himself has memorized more of Scripture than most of us, but he hates it and uses it for malign purposes to undermine God's program of salvation. We must do more than sing:

Holy Book book divine,
Precious treasure, thou art mine.

We must make the Word of God the searchlight that scans our hearts to convict us of sin and brings us to a place of confession and restoration, after which we must carefully walk in obedience to all of its precepts and commandments. Let there be no blank pages in our Bibles!

PRAYER

We have linked Bible study and prayer together. As we have said, God talks to us through Scripture. We talk to God through prayer. Prayer consists in five parts—adoration, thanksgiving, confession, petition, and intercession. We should always precede petition and intercession with adoration, thanksgiving, and confession. Adoration consists in the worship of God and who he is; thanksgiving consists in the expression of gratitude for the manifold blessings of God which he has bestowed upon us day by day in salvation and the common blessings of life. Confession consists in telling God what things we have failed to do, and what deeds we have done imperfectly. We ask forgiveness for our sins. And we freely receive God's pardon and thank him for the forgiveness he promises to all who confess their sins to him.

Petition and intercession consist in asking God for our own personal and immediate family needs and for the needs of others. Such prayers should include friends, relatives, missionaries, and the host of other individuals, works, agencies, and organizations which need intercession. God invites us to present our petitions and intercessions and agrees to hear them and to answer them for us. Whatever promises God makes in his Word, we can claim in faith and expect him to fulfill each and every one of them. He is a gentleman who always keeps his word. For things which are not specifically promised we may have to append the words "if it be thy will." In some items for which there is no specific biblical promise the Holy Spirit may give us the gift of faith to believe that God will grant this or that request.

A number of books have been written on the subject of prayer. We should use this devotional material to learn about the laws which govern prayer, the hindrances to effective praying, and the thousands of illustrations of how God has answered prayers for his people through the ages. I wrote a book *When You Pray* which has been a blessing to many people.

We do not need to go into further detail about prayer at this point. But we must understand that none of us can live an effective life before God without making use of prayer. If we are living as we ought, prayer will be an important component of our lives. Paul has left us a number of injunctions and promises in connection with prayer. Thus he said: "Pray without ceasing" (1 Thess. 5:17). He also said:

> Let your moderation be known unto all men. The Lord is at hand. Be careful for nothing; but in everything by prayer and supplication with thanksgiving let your requests be made known to God. And the peace of God which passeth all understanding, shall keep your hearts and minds through Christ Jesus [Phil. 4:5-7].

The word which has been recorded in connection with the teaching of Jesus is paramount to all of our discussion. Luke wrote: "And he [Jesus] spake a parable unto them to this end, that men ought always to pray, and not to faint" (Luke 18:1). Here Jesus places his seal of approval on prayer as such. What characterized his life should characterize ours. He prayed and we should follow his example. We are to follow in his steps. Prayer is not to be secondary but primary. We are *always* to pray. Nothing is excluded from prayer, and no matter is too trivial to be brought to God's attention. And we are to persevere in prayer. We are not to faint, according to Jesus. This suggests that prayer may indeed be a difficult pursuit which will demand all that we have and leave us tired and weary. But we are not to faint. We must stay with our prayers until they are answered and God is glorified in those answers.

The sorrowful words of Jesus in Gethsemane's Garden should be written on the fleshy tables of our hearts. He was praying and his disciples had long since fallen asleep. The bloody beads of perspiration were dropping from the furrowed brow of our Lord. When he had finished his prayer, he said to Peter: "What, could ye not watch with me one hour? Watch and pray, that ye enter not into temptation: the spirit indeed is willing, but the flesh is weak" (Matt. 26:40, 41). Watch and pray! These are Jesus' admonitions for us as we wait for his coming.

WITNESSING

The fully rounded Christian life must include sharing with others what God in Jesus Christ has done for you and me. Irrespective of our vocational calling, we are all enjoined to tell others wherever we are that Jesus is the Savior of the world. The command of Jesus constitutes the divine call to witnessing:

> But ye shall receive power, after that the Holy Ghost is come upon you: and ye shall be witnesses unto me both in Jerusalem, and in all Judaea, and in Samaria, and unto the uttermost part of the earth [Acts 1:8].

God does not call all of us to go to the ends of the earth. But he does call for the Church to do so, which means that some of its members must respond to this part of the call. But when he said to his disciples that they were to begin at Jerusalem, he left behind the basic injunction that, like them, we are to witness *where we are*—on the farm, in the big city, in suburbia, or wherever we may be. Some may, like Solzhenitsyn, hear the witness of a Christian in the Gulag Archipelago. Some may hear it in the noisy factories of Detroit. Some may hear it over the fence from a neighboring housewife hanging wash on the line. Some may hear it on TV or the radio. Some may hear it in the local grog shop. Some may hear it from a physician or a nurse while lying on a hospital bed.

The Scripture says that "the gospel must first be published among all the nations" (Mark 13:10). Only then will the end come. We are to hasten the day of the coming of the Lord Jesus by finishing the task of world evangelization. Until that is accomplished, Jesus will not come. How are we to fulfill the terms of this commandment of Jesus? We are to go, to give, and to pray.

Going implies that we must acquire adequate knowledge which we are to transmit to those who do not know Jesus. We do not need to be theological experts. All we need to do is share with others what Jesus Christ has done for us after learning the few basic laws of salvation. Some people have made light of Campus Crusade's *Four Spiritual Laws*. Probably many of those who laugh at what they think is a simplistic approach do not witness often, if ever. Many of us have found in these four laws a handle we can latch onto to help us do the work of effective witnessing. No one is limited to this method. Anyone who develops a more comprehensive and effective method of witnessing should be appreciated and encouraged. How we do it is not as important as doing it. Sometimes the Holy Spirit uses the most unexpected and apparently ineffective ways to bring sinners into the Kingdom. Somewhere in the process of witnessing we must let people know they are sinners, they are lost, they need a Savior, God loves them and has made provision for their salvation, Jesus has finished the work of salvation on the cross of Calvary, and they need to repent and receive Jesus into their hearts. These truths constitute the basics for biblical evangelism. When people are saved they can quickly learn other doctrines of the Christian faith. Being saved is only the beginning. There must be the work of conservation in which converts are shepherded and watched over as babies are nurtured by their mothers and fathers. The key word which follows witnessing is follow-up.

Since all of us cannot go to the ends of the earth, our obligation is not fulfilled when we have witnessed where we are. We must give and pray for the lost, and for those who seek to reach them by going to the ends of the earth. There has never yet been a live church which was not an evangelistic and a missionary church. Wherever theological liberalism creeps into a church, evangelism and missions take a nosedive. So giving and praying are called for on the part of those who cannot go but who by their gifts and their prayers send others to the uttermost parts of our planet. Daniel wrote:

> And many of them that sleep in the dust of the earth shall awake, some to everlasting life, and some to shame and everlasting contempt. And they that be wise shall shine as the brightness of the firmament; and *they that turn many to righteousness* as the stars for ever and ever [Daniel 12:2, 3, italics added].

How then shall we live while we wait for the coming of the Lord? We must accept that which God has called us to and, by discharging these obligations, we will glorify God and enjoy him forever. We are to watch while we wait. And we are to work while we watch. Idleness and sloth are sins against God. The church at Thessalonica thought the day of the Lord had come. The members were sitting idly on their hands, doing nothing except gossiping and being busybodies. Paul rebuked them sharply when he said:

> Now them that are such we command and exhort by our Lord Jesus Christ, that with quietness they work, and eat their own bread. But ye, brethren, be not weary in well doing. And if any man obey not our word by this epistle, note that man, and have no company with him, that he may be ashamed. Yet count him not as an enemy, but admonish him as a brother [2 Thess. 3:12-15].

LIVING IN THE LIGHT OF THE RAPTURE

How we are to live must be looked at in connection with the rapture of the Church. Those who accept the pretribulationist view stress the need for special concern to live the Christian life to the fullest degree because of the nearness of Christ's coming for his Church. A. C. Gaebelein painted a picture for this viewpoint in the words:

> If the church were to pass through the tribulation period all the exhortation to wait for the Coming of the Lord, to watch for Him, to be ready would have no meaning. It would be more correct to exhort to wait for the coming of the beast. The blessed hope to meet Him would lose its blessedness. Instead of being a bright outlook to be with Christ in glory, it would be the worst pessimism, for believers would not face immediate glory, but tribulation, judgments, and the persecutions of the beast from the pit. Everything in Scripture is against this teaching, which has been accepted by not a few, that the church must pass through the tribulation, and after all it is an important truth for the spiritual life of a believer. If the Lord cannot come for His Saints till the Roman empire is again in existence, and the two beasts have made their appearance to do their work, if He cannot come till the Jews are back in Palestine and have rebuilt their temple, *then the real power of that blessed hope in the daily life of the Christian is gone. The danger then is to say, "My Lord delays His coming," and with it drift into worldly ways* [my italics]. [Studies in Prophecy, N.Y., 1918, p. 73, 74.]

Dr. Gaebelein correctly notes that the imminence of the rapture as popularly conceived would be nonviable if post-tribulationism is true, and that the members of Christ's Church would have to wait for the coming of the Antichrist, persecution, and martyrdom. Therefore he concludes that such a scenario would take away the real power of the blessed hope and change the attitude of the believer detrimentally. He goes so far as to say that the people of God would be in danger of "drifting into worldly ways." Thus the pretribulational rapture keeps God's people from drifting into worldly ways.

If the posttribulational view is correct, and that is the real question, it is hard to believe that the consequences would be as devastating as Dr. Gaebelein predicts. One must note that there is a certain amount of circular reasoning contained in Dr. Gaebelein's appeal. He is saying that since these evil consequences would flow from rejecting the pretribulational view, this somehow validates that viewpoint. This is a non sequitur. The only question is whether the Scripture teaches posttribulationism or not. If it does, then the consequences flowing out of that teaching must be looked at squarely and openly. On the other hand, if the pretribulational view does prove to be incorrect, then the holder of that view would be most unprepared for having to go through the tribulation, and his faith might indeed be shaken and his life damaged.

Is it not rather that Scripture lays before us the kind of life the believer is to lead regardless of anything else—be it a rapture which precedes the tribulation or a rapture which comes at the end of the tribulation? And would not a pretribulational rapture lessen the concern of the Church for evangelism of the world when this view holds that the Jews will do in seven years by way of evangelization what the Church has not been able to do for twenty centuries? And they will do it with far fewer people than the Church and with the presence of the Holy Spirit withdrawn.

Dr. Gaebelein creates an even greater problem which should not be overlooked lightly. After the Church has been raptured and the tribulation begins, the believing Jews will evangelize the world, that is the world of Gentiles. He wrote:

> We learn that this great multitude of all nations comes out of the Great Tribulation. It is not the Church, for the

Church is not in the Great Tribulation. This great multitude represents the Gentile nations who heard the final
testimony and who believed. They turned in repentance
to God and were then washed in the Blood of the Lamb.
... They are the nations which the King calls blessed,
and which will inherit the Kingdom.

We now discover that there are three classes of people
instead of the two of which he generally speaks. We have
Israel, the Church, and the tribulation saints. The tribulation
saints are certainly not Jews and he says they are not in the
Church. Here are three peoples of God. As if this were not
enough, he still has the problem of what to do with the Gentiles who were saved in the Old Testament. They are not Israel,
nor can they be the Church, according to his pattern. Do they
constitute a fourth class of people? They certainly cannot be
identified as having come out of the great tribulation to inherit
the Kingdom. But does not the Kingdom in Dr. Gaebelein's
view belong to the Jews? Does this mean there is a Jewish kingdom and a Gentile kingdom? If Dr. Gaebelein includes them in
Israel, then the term Israel must be extended to include Gentiles. In that event, why not include the Church also? If Dr.
Gaebelein places them in the Church, then part of the Church
will go through the tribulation. If he leaves them out of both
groups, he has an unresolved mystery.

Dr. Scofield goes even further than Dr. Gaebelein, for he
distinguishes between "my gospel" of the Apostle Paul and
the everlasting gospel of the tribulation period. He wrote: "It
is neither the Gospel of the kingdom, nor of grace."

Dr. Scofield and Dr. Gaebelein seem to contradict each other.
If Dr. Scofield is right, that these Gentiles do not hear the
gospel of the kingdom, then the kingdom of which Dr. Gaebelein speaks cannot be theirs. If it is not the gospel of grace,
what is it? And are not all men saved by grace through all ages?

The midtribulationist would warn the Church to be ready for
the onslaught of the wrath of man which it must endure. This
period will last for three and a half years. Some of God's saints
will be martyred and those who live will suffer. But at the end
of this period, the Church will be caught away before the wrath
of God is poured out on the world. This means that the coming
of the rapture is imminent but that certain prophecies must

be fulfilled before the Church departs. Since the rapture could not have taken place a thousand years ago, and since men like Dr. Gaebelein and Dr. Scofield agree, why would not church people a thousand years ago say, "My Lord delays his coming?" Why is the danger today different from the danger of drifting into worldly living a millennium ago?

The psychological advantage seems to lie with the posttribulational position. The holders of this view warn that the Church must face the wrath of man. Therefore, the Church must be prepared and is called upon to live according to God's plan despite whatever happens. When the wrath of God is poured out, it is safe to conclude that God will preserve his people from that wrath even as he kept the Israelites from the effects of the plagues which he poured out on the Egyptians. Moreover, the verse "For God hath not appointed us to wrath, but to obtain salvation by our Lord Jesus Christ" cannot be understood only one way. It can mean that we escape the final wrath of God which is poured out in the final judgment. Since we have been appointed to salvation through Jesus Christ, we escape that wrath which is to come. To claim that this verse means we escape wrath by a pretribulational rapture does not necessarily follow. At best it is questionable and certainly not a verse on which to rest the pretribulational case. The psychological advantage of the posttribulational position is this: if the position is correct, the Church is prepared for what it will have to endure and nothing is lost; if the position is incorrect and the Church is raptured before the tribulation the posttribulationists have everything to gain. They will escape what they thought they had to go through and will praise God and be relieved. But the pretribulationists, if they are wrong, will have lost everything they hold dear. Is it not safer, then, to be discreet and hold in abeyance any dogmatic endorsement of any of the three possible positions? But this much we do know —how we should live until Christ raptures the Church and returns in glory.

The words of the Apostle Paul are appropriate and apply beautifully as a summary of how we should live:

> Another reason for right living is this: you know how late it is; time is running out. Wake up, for the coming of the Lord is nearer now than when we first believed. The night

is far gone, the day of his return will soon be here. So quit the evil deeds of darkness and put on the armor of right living, as we who live in the daylight should! Be decent and true in everything you do so that all can approve your behavior. Don't spend your time in wild parties and getting drunk or in adultery and lust, or fighting, or jealousy. But ask the Lord Jesus to help you live as you should, and don't make plans to enjoy evil [Rom. 13:11-14, TLB].

The Lord *is* coming. But until he does come to catch away the Church, every member of that body should be about the Lord's business. Our hearts and our houses should be clean. Our accounts should be up-to-date. Our prayers should be fully said. Our witnessing should be current. Our beings should be filled with the Holy Spirit. And our lips should be framing the words: "Even so, come, Lord Jesus."